Texas Tables

Texas Tables

The Junior League of North Harris and
South Montgomery Counties, Inc.

Photography by Terry Vine
Food Styling by Julie Hettiger

Texas Tables

Published by The Junior League of North Harris and South Montgomery Counties, Inc.
Copyright © 2010

**THE JUNIOR LEAGUE OF NORTH HARRIS
AND SOUTH MONTGOMERY COUNTIES, INC.**
Women building better communities®

The Junior League of North Harris and South Montgomery Counties, Inc.
21021 Springbrook Plaza Drive, Suite 175
Spring, Texas 77379
281.376.5754

Food Photography: © Terry Vine
Food Stylist: Julie Hettiger

The Texas produce sidebars in *Texas Tables* are referenced from www.picktexas.com,
The Texas Department of Agriculture.

Library of Congress Number: 2009927733
ISBN: 978-0-9657063-1-5

Edited, Designed and Produced by

 Favorite Recipes® Press

An imprint of

FRP.INC

A wholly owned subsidiary of Southwestern/Great American, Inc.
P.O. Box 305142
Nashville, Tennessee 37230
800.358.0560

Editorial Director: Mary Cummings
Art Director and Book Design: Steve Newman
Project Manager and Editor: Debbie Van Mol

Manufactured in the United States of America
First Printing: 2010
20,000 copies

For additional copies of
Texas Tables
or for order information on any of the League's cookbooks, please contact
The Junior League of North Harris and South Montgomery Counties, Inc.
To order on line, visit our Web site at www.JLNHSMC.org, or call 888.TEX.TIES.

 Texas Tables is printed on recycled paper with 10 percent post-consumer waste.

May your tables be crafted with patience,
develop character with time,
be set with grace,
and be surrounded by warmth and love.

From Our Table to Yours

Texas Tables was created for everyone who loves to share good food with family and friends around a table. In Texas, tables are cherished as a place where traditions are created with special meals during celebrations, holiday gatherings, and family dinners. Our affection for the table goes beyond the dining room; recall the many important moments in your life, and how so many of them happened gathered around the breakfast table, the patio table or even the coffee table.

From laughter to tears to life-changing decisions, the tables in our homes hold so many of our most special memories. My fondest memory as a child was the celebration of a "Birthday Breakfast," where my mother set the table with fine linens, china, and crystal and prepared a delicious breakfast for each child's birthday. I have continued that same tradition today with my own family. One League member referred to her dining table as a "lovely lady" for the way it stands so graceful and elegant, reigning over the home. We hope this book makes you reflect on the role your "lovely lady" has in your home and in the lives of your family.

Texas Tables is the second published cookbook for our League. Our first cookbook, the award-winning Texas Ties, was developed based on the idea that food, specifically comfort foods, can be shared with family and friends. Texas Tables continues in the same spirit as Texas Ties. The connections and ties we have made with our family and friends while enjoying good food can be shared around the table. Whether it is an old table that brings back memories of the past or a new table that allows opportunities for establishing new traditions, Texas Tables presents you with a collection of recipes that create excitement around any table.

We received more than 1,300 recipes from members of The Junior League of North Harris and South Montgomery Counties, Inc., including recipes from family, friends, and several local chefs. Every single recipe was thoroughly tested and critiqued by the members and friends of the League before being selected for this book. We would like to thank each person who contributed, cooked, tested, and tasted recipes for Texas Tables. This has given us the opportunity to present a wonderful book of food, unique table settings, stories relating interesting facts and tales about people, places, and events, and photography that captures the genre of food. We hope you enjoy Texas Tables and that it will be shared by generations from years to come.

Shannon Thornton Mills

Shannon Thornton Mills
President 2009–2010

Introduction

We invite you with warmth and in friendship to the tables of the women of The Junior League of North Harris and South Montgomery Counties, Inc. We present you with recipes that are well-tested for your pleasure to share with your family and friends as they gather around your own table. We share with you memories, stories, and histories of our lives through tables, sharing the best of times and what makes us special.

Our Junior League service area lies in the natural regions of Texas in what are known as the Gulf Coast Plains and the Piney Woods of East Texas. Blessed with a long growing season, both regions are rich in agriculture and ranching, offering an abundance of fresh fruits and vegetables most of the year as well as a wide variety of meats and fish from the Gulf. Encompassing Northwest Houston, The Woodlands, and the surrounding communities, our region boasts a rich cultural life, including museums, theatre, music, movies, oil and gas, business, and some of the top medical centers in the world. The Gulf Coast Plains and the Piney Woods regions have lakes, pine trees, and plenty of sunshine and warm weather, with something beautiful in bloom year-round. Though many of us are from the area, even more of us have been transplanted here and bring more culture and diversity to us.

It is with pride that we share our abundances with you in *Texas Tables*. You are about to embark on a journey that will take you down a path of culinary delights, personal stories of table memories and traditions, clever and timely tips on cooking, and gorgeous pictures to set the mood of gathering with friends and family to reminisce of the past or create new memories. *Texas Tables* was inspired by the feelings, memories, and lifetime of emotions associated with a constant, yet almost invisible, gathering spot in most homes—the table. The table boldly stands on strong legs patiently waiting for attention during the very busy, fast-paced lives of today and holding onto the calm that comforts us when we do finally sit down together.

Table, derived from the Latin word "tabula" meaning "board," is the foundation on which we spread our feasts and share the special moments in our lives. In Grecian history, tables were a simple slab of wood set on legs set up for the purposes of meals, then vanishing immediately along with the empty plates. The Romans, on the other hand, collected tables, a penchant to their love of luxury, but not necessarily used for the purposes of gathering to dine. It wasn't until the medieval times that families came together at a "dining" table with the sincere intent to share a meal. While the four-legged kind are most common, make-shift tables are set regularly on patio summer kitchens, picnic blankets, even lounge chairs by the pool. The table symbolically is a place to gather, and we make the most of that translation. Imagine the journey the tables in your home have made and the stories each could tell if they could speak.

For where there are people, there are tables and food—it is the "holy trinity" of entertaining. Consider the words of the hymn, "We Come to Your Feast," by Michael Joncas as you move forward through *Texas Tables*.

We place upon your table a gleaming cloth of white: the weaving of our stories, the fabric of our lives;
    the dreams of those before us, the ancient hopeful cries,
    the promise of our future: our needing and our nurture lie here before our eyes.
We gather 'round your table, we pause within our quest, we stand beside our neighbors,
    we name the stranger 'guest.' The feast is spread before us; you bid us come and dine:
    in blessing we'll uncover, in sharing we'll discover your substance and your sign.

Welcome to our tables—our *Texas Tables*. You are our guest. We hope you will enjoy our League's very best recipes and the graciousness of our region with all of its warmth, so that you may, too, create your very own feasts for those most precious to you. *Wishing everyone a bountiful table surrounded by family and friends.*

Contents of Our Table

The Breakfast Tray

Nothing quite delivers a feeling of warmth and comfort like the aroma of breakfast and freshly brewed coffee. Whether it's a simple dish of fruit and toast to send us on our way each day or an elaborate brunch spread for a special occasion, breakfast is a favorite repast in Texas. As the morning sun shines through our tall pine trees of eastern Texas, hunger moves us toward the breakfast table, and we start to anticipate the event of the coming day.

While a brunch table, set with endless possibilities of culinary delights, embodies all the optimism and hope of each family gathering and special event, it is the time at the breakfast table, shared in the quiet morning hours with those closest to us, that eases us into the dawn of each new day.

"Life, within doors, has few pleasanter prospects than a neatly arranged and well-provisioned breakfast table."

—Nathaniel Hawthorne

Asparagus Chicken Quiche	16	26	Blueberry Bread
Perfect Breakfast Pie	18	26	Chocolate Chunk Banana Bread
Eggs Benedict with Southwestern Hollandaise Sauce	19	28	Pear Preserve Bread
Pecan Waffles with Banana Syrup	21	28	Pumpkin Butterscotch Muffins
French Toast Baked in Grand Marnier	22	29	Morning Glory Muffins
Apple Buttermilk Pancakes	22	29	Easy Overnight Cinnamon Rolls
Glazed Comstock Bacon	23	30	Family Favorite Cinnamon Rolls
Hash Brown Strata	23	32	Cherry Almond Scones
Iron Skillet Almond Cake	24	33	Honey Puff
Mixed Berry Galette	24		

Asparagus Chicken Quiche

8 (or more) asparagus spears
Salt to taste
1 refrigerated pie pastry or
    homemade pie pastry

2 tablespoons chopped chives or
    green onion tops
4 slices bacon
3/4 cup chopped cooked chicken
    or turkey
3 eggs, beaten

1 1/2 cups milk
1/8 teaspoon salt
1/8 teaspoon pepper
1 1/2 cups (6 ounces) shredded
    sharp Cheddar cheese
1 tablespoon all-purpose flour

Blanching

Blanching is another term for parboiling, or lightly cooking, ingredients— usually vegetables—in boiling water until just tender. The ingredients are then rinsed under ice cold water and drained. This stops the cooking process. Blanching helps vegetables keep their texture and color and also removes bitterness.

Preheat the oven to 450 degrees. Break off the woody ends of the asparagus spears; the spears should be approximately 4 1/2 inches long. Cook the asparagus in boiling salted water in a saucepan for 5 minutes; drain. Immediately plunge the asparagus into a bowl of ice water to stop the cooking process; drain.

Unfold the refrigerated pie pastry on a lightly floured surface and gently press the chives into the pastry. If preparing homemade pie pastry, roll the pastry into a 13-inch circle on a lightly floured surface and gently press the chives into the pastry. Fit the pastry into a 10-inch quiche dish or rectangular tart pan and trim the edges. Gently pierce the pastry with a wooden pick or small skewer. Line the pastry with a double thickness of heavy-duty foil. Bake for 6 to 7 minutes or until the pastry is set and dry. Remove from the oven. Reduce the oven temperature to 350 degrees.

Cook the bacon in a skillet until crisp. Drain, reserving the bacon drippings in the skillet. Crumble the bacon. Sauté the chicken in the reserved bacon drippings; drain.

Combine the eggs, milk, 1/8 teaspoon salt and the pepper in a bowl and stir until blended. Stir in the bacon and chicken. Toss the cheese and flour in a small bowl and sprinkle over the bottom of the hot crust. Pour the egg mixture over the cheese.

Arrange the asparagus in a spoke pattern over the top or with the spears facing the same direction. Bake for 55 to 60 minutes or until a knife inserted near the center comes out clean. Let stand for 10 to 15 minutes before serving. Leftovers may be reheated. Serves 6 to 8.

Photograph for this recipe on facing page.

Perfect Breakfast Pie

1 unbaked (9-inch) pie shell
1 pound ground hot breakfast
    pork sausage or lean
    pork sausage
1 tablespoon butter

1/2 cup chopped onion
3/4 cup milk
3 ounces cream cheese, cubed
1/4 cup chopped peeled roasted
    poblano pepper
3 eggs

1 cup (4 ounces) shredded white
    Cheddar cheese
3/4 teaspoon Worcestershire sauce
1/4 teaspoon salt
1/8 teaspoon freshly ground pepper

Pie Pans

Baking 9- to 10-inch pies is best done in heatproof glass pans. Not only does the glass allow you to visually determine when the crust has browned to your satisfaction, but it also holds heat which then penetrates the crust thoroughly. The result is a dryer, deeper crust. Those shiny, white ceramic pans, while beautiful, reflect the heat instead of absorbing it and do not bake as effectively.

Preheat the oven to 350 degrees. Bake the pie shell for 8 minutes; the pie shell will be partially baked. Let stand until cool. Increase the oven temperature to 375 degrees.

Brown the sausage in a skillet, stirring until crumbly; drain. Wipe the skillet with a paper towel. Melt the butter in the skillet over medium heat and add the onion. Sauté until the onion is tender. Stir in the milk and cook just until steam begins to rise. Remove from the heat and immediately stir in the cream cheese and poblano pepper.

Whisk the eggs in a bowl until combined. Stir the eggs, cheese, Worcestershire sauce, salt and pepper into the cream cheese mixture. Pour into the pie shell and top with the sausage. Bake for 50 to 60 minutes or until set, covering loosely with foil if needed to prevent overbrowning. You may prepare up to 2 days in advance and store, covered, in the refrigerator. Reheat just before serving. Serves 6 to 8.

My kitchen table embarrasses my son to no end. It is an antique farm table that we rescued from someone's trash one day. My husband used the excuse that he needed a table for his workshop and asked to take it. The table was missing a drawer and had lime green legs. After refinishing it and building a new drawer, we have used it for twenty-four years. There are even a few splatters of paint from the kids' art projects, but we still love it. Shortly after we refinished the table, we found one identical to it for $800 while antiquing in Pennsylvania, so we loved it even more. —J. Jewell

Eggs Benedict with
Southwestern Hollandaise Sauce

Southwestern Hollandaise Sauce
1/2 cup (1 stick) butter or
    clarified butter
3 egg yolks
2 to 6 tablespoons hot water
1 1/2 tablespoons fresh lemon juice
1 teaspoon adobo sauce, drained
    from canned chipotle peppers

Pinch of salt
Pinch of pepper
1 teaspoon chopped cilantro

Eggs Benedict
1 poblano pepper
1/2 teaspoon cayenne pepper
4 slices Canadian bacon

2 English muffins, split into halves
Butter to taste
2 tablespoons white vinegar
4 eggs
4 sprigs of cilantro

Preheat the oven to the broiler setting.

For the sauce, melt the butter in a small saucepan; do not allow to brown. Bring a small saucepan with water to a low boil and place a stainless steel bowl over the pan or use a double boiler. Whisk the eggs in the stainless steel bowl until combined and place the bowl over the simmering water. Add 2 tablespoons of the hot water, the lemon juice, adobo sauce, salt and pepper to the eggs. Simmer for 2 minutes or until foamy, whisking constantly and removing the bowl from the simmering water if it begins to get too hot; do not allow the eggs to cook. Add additional hot water as needed and simmer for 5 minutes or until thickened. Add the melted butter gradually, whisking constantly. Continue to cook, whisking constantly; the sauce should double in volume. Turn off the heat and stir in the cilantro. Taste and season as desired. Cover the bowl with plastic wrap until ready for use. Add a small amount of hot water and lightly whisk if the sauce separates. Do not reheat over direct heat.

For the eggs Benedict, roast the poblano pepper directly over an open flame until the pepper is charred on all sides. Place in a sealable plastic bag and let stand until cool. Remove the charred skin and seeds from the pepper under running water. Cut the pepper into quarters. Rub the cayenne pepper over the Canadian bacon slices. Heat the Canadian bacon slightly in a nonstick skillet. Brush the cut sides of the muffins with butter and arrange on a baking sheet. Broil until light brown. Add the vinegar to a medium stockpot filled with water and bring almost to a boil. Crack the eggs directly into the water. Poach for about 2 to 4 minutes or until the whites are no longer translucent. Remove the eggs to a platter using a slotted spoon. If the eggs do not coagulate, add additional vinegar to the water and repeat the process with additional eggs. To serve, layer the muffin halves evenly with the poblano pepper, Canadian bacon and eggs on serving plates. Drizzle with the sauce and top each with a sprig of cilantro. Serve immediately. Serves 2 to 4.

Photograph for this recipe on page 13.

Breakfast for Dinner

In Texas we often use the saying, "Breakfast is good any time of the day." Considered a comfort meal, try serving a full breakfast at dinner time. Perfect for a fall or winter night! Or, as many Texans believe, any time of the year.

Pecan Waffles with Banana Syrup

Banana Syrup
1/2 cup (1 stick) butter
1/2 cup pecan pieces, lightly toasted
1 cup good-quality dark amber
    maple syrup
2 bananas, cut into 1/4-inch slices

Pecan Waffles
2 cups all-purpose flour
1/2 cup pecan pieces, lightly toasted
11/2 teaspoons baking powder
1/4 teaspoon salt
4 egg yolks

1/4 to 1/2 cup granulated sugar
21/2 cups milk
1/2 cup (1 stick) butter, melted
1 teaspoon vanilla extract
4 egg whites
Confectioners' sugar to taste

*P*reheat the oven to 200 degrees.

For the syrup, bring the butter, pecans, maple syrup and bananas to a simmer in a sauté pan, stirring frequently. Remove from the heat and cover to keep warm.

For the waffles, mix the flour, pecans, baking powder and salt in a bowl. Combine the egg yolks and granulated sugar in a bowl and whisk until combined. Add the milk, butter and vanilla and whisk until blended. Add the flour mixture and stir just until combined; do not overmix. Beat the egg whites in a mixing bowl until soft peaks form. Fold the egg whites into the batter. Bake in a waffle iron using the manufacturer's directions; each waffle takes about 4 to 6 minutes. Keep warm in the oven. To serve, sprinkle confectioners' sugar over the waffles and drizzle with the syrup. For variety, omit the pecans from the batter and add chopped crystallized ginger or omit the bananas from the syrup. Serves 6.

Photograph for this recipe on facing page.

*M*y kitchen table belonged to my grandmother, and it conjures up great memories. I remember her uptown New Orleans "shot gun" house (the house travels from front to back one room at a time ending with the kitchen, the busiest and largest room in her home). The focal point was her kitchen table, a large, well-worn oak table with sturdy legs and clawed feet resembling a lion's. Mornings would start with bacon, eggs, and biscuits. Lunch was seafood gumbo or étouffée, and then boiled seafood was for dinner, complete with piles of crabs laid out on newspaper in the center of the table. Cracking the claws by hammering them on the table upset no one! Now the table belongs to my family . . . it has been refinished, but many of the memories are still contained in its wooden top. My youngest daughter still ponders the lion-clawed feet. I hope the memories my children will have will show the love shared around that table throughout the generations!   —T. Johnson

French Toast Baked in Grand Marnier

1 cup packed brown sugar
1/2 cup (1 stick) unsalted butter
2 tablespoons corn syrup

8 (1-inch) slices French bread
1 1/2 cups half-and-half
5 eggs
1/4 cup Grand Marnier

1 teaspoon vanilla extract
1/4 teaspoon salt
1/4 cup pecans, chopped

This recipe requires 8 hours of refrigeration. Preheat the oven to 350 degrees. Heat the brown sugar, butter and corn syrup in a saucepan until the brown sugar melts, stirring frequently. Pour into a 9×13-inch baking pan, tilting the pan to ensure even coverage. Arrange the bread slices over the prepared layer.

Whisk the half-and-half, eggs, liqueur, vanilla and salt in a bowl until blended. Stir in the pecans and pour over the bread. Chill, covered, for 8 to 24 hours. Let stand until room temperature. Bake, uncovered, for 35 to 40 minutes or until puffed and golden brown. Serves 8.

Apple Buttermilk Pancakes

2 cups all-purpose flour
1/4 cup sugar
1 teaspoon baking soda

1/4 teaspoon salt
2 Granny Smith apples, peeled
    and chopped
2 tablespoons butter

2 cups buttermilk
2 tablespoons butter, melted
2 eggs

Mix the flour, sugar, baking soda and salt in a bowl. Sauté the apples in 2 tablespoons butter in a skillet until soft but not mushy. Whisk the buttermilk, 2 tablespoons melted butter and the eggs in a bowl until blended. Add the buttermilk mixture to the dry ingredients and stir just until combined. Fold in the apples.

Pour approximately 1/4 cup of the batter onto a hot lightly greased griddle. Bake until bubbles appear on the surface and the underside is golden brown. Turn the pancake. Be careful not to press on the pancake as this will pop the bubbles and yield a denser pancake. Cook until the remaining side is golden brown. Repeat the process with the remaining batter. Serves 2 to 4.

Glazed Comstock Bacon

1 to 2 cups packed dark
    brown sugar

1 to 2 pounds thick-sliced bacon
1 teaspoon cayenne pepper

Preheat the oven to 425 degrees. Line one or two baking pans with baking parchment. Sprinkle enough brown sugar over the bacon to coat, pressing to ensure the brown sugar adheres. Sprinkle with the cayenne pepper.

Arrange the bacon in a single layer in the prepared baking pans. Bake for 15 to 20 minutes or until the bacon is crisp. Immediately remove the bacon to a wire rack placed over paper towels. Serves 10 to 12.

Photograph for this recipe on page 13.

Hash Brown Strata

1 (24-ounce) package frozen
    shredded hash brown
    potatoes, thawed
Olive oil
1 cup (4 ounces) shredded
    jalapeño cheese

1 cup (4 ounces) shredded
    Monterey Jack cheese
1 cup chopped cooked ham
1/2 cup milk
1/3 cup butter, melted
2 eggs

1/4 teaspoon seasoned salt
1 Roma tomato, seeded and
    coarsely chopped
4 basil leaves, chiffonade

Preheat the oven to 350 degrees. Lightly brown the potatoes in olive oil in a sauté pan. Press the potatoes over the bottom of a greased 9-inch pie plate or tart pan. Sprinkle with the cheese and ham.

Whisk the milk, butter, eggs and salt in a bowl until blended and pour over the prepared layers. Bake for 30 to 40 minutes or until a knife inserted in the center comes out clean, arranging the tomatoes over the top in a decorative pattern and sprinkling with the basil during the last 10 minutes of the baking process. Let stand for 5 minutes before serving. Serves 6.

Iron Skillet Almond Cake

3/4 cup (1 1/2 sticks) plus
1 tablespoon butter
(no substitutions)

3 eggs
1 1/2 cups granulated sugar
1 1/2 cups sifted all-purpose flour
1 teaspoon almond flavoring

Dash of salt
All-purpose flour
1/4 cup slivered almonds
Confectioners' sugar to taste

Preheat the oven to 350 degrees. Melt the butter in a 10-inch cast-iron skillet. Whisk the eggs in a large bowl until blended. Add the granulated sugar, 1 1/2 cups flour, the flavoring and salt; mix until combined. Stir in the melted butter. Coat the cast-iron skillet lightly with flour and pour the batter into the skillet. Sprinkle with the almonds. Bake for 30 minutes or until the cake begins to pull from the side of the skillet. Do not overbake. Immediately wrap the cake in foil to keep moist. Dust with confectioners' sugar before serving. Serve with fresh fruit. Serves 8 to 10.

Mixed Berry Galette

1/3 cup ice water
3 tablespoons sour cream
1 cup plus 2 tablespoons
all-purpose flour
1/4 cup cornmeal

1 1/2 tablespoons granulated sugar
1/2 teaspoon salt
8 tablespoons butter, chilled and
cut into small pieces
1 1/2 cups mixed berries (no
strawberries)

2 tablespoons granulated sugar
1 tablespoon honey
Egg wash (1 lightly beaten egg and
2 tablespoons milk)
Coarse sugar to taste

This recipe requires 2 hours of refrigeration. Preheat the oven to 350 degrees. Mix the ice water and sour cream in a bowl. Place the flour, cornmeal, 1 1/2 tablespoons granulated sugar and the salt in a food processor and pulse to combine. Add 7 tablespoons of the butter, pulsing constantly until the mixture resembles peas. Add the sour cream mixture and pulse just until combined; scrape the side of the bowl. Wrap the dough in plastic wrap and chill for 2 hours or longer; the dough will look wet. Toss the berries with 2 tablespoons granulated sugar, remaining 1 tablespoon butter and the honey in a bowl. Roll the chilled dough into a 1/4-inch-thick round on a lightly floured piece of baking parchment. Place the baking parchment and dough round on a baking sheet. Spoon the berry filling in the center of the round. Fold the dough about 1 inch over the filling. Brush with egg wash and sprinkle with coarse sugar. Bake for 25 to 35 minutes or until golden brown. Serves 4.

Photograph for this recipe on facing page.

Blueberry Bread

2 3/4 cups all-purpose flour
1 cup sugar
1 tablespoon baking powder
1/2 teaspoon baking soda
1/2 teaspoon salt

1 cup buttermilk
1 cup (2 sticks) butter, melted
3 eggs
1 tablespoon vanilla extract
3 cups fresh blueberries

1/2 cup sugar
1/4 cup all-purpose flour
1/2 cup (1 stick) butter, chilled and
    cut into small pieces
1/2 teaspoon cinnamon

Preheat the oven to 350 degrees. Sift 2 3/4 cups flour, 1 cup sugar, the baking powder, baking soda and salt together onto a sheet of waxed paper. Whisk the buttermilk, 1 cup butter, the eggs and vanilla in a bowl until blended. Add the flour mixture and mix just until blended. Pour the batter evenly into two buttered and floured 4×9-inch loaf pans. Sprinkle with the blueberries. Combine 1/2 cup sugar, 1/4 cup flour, 1/2 cup butter and 1/2 teaspoon cinnamon in a bowl and mix until crumbly using a pastry blender. Sprinkle the crumb mixture over the blueberries. Bake for 45 to 50 minutes or until a knife inserted in the centers comes out clean. Cool in the pans for 10 minutes. Remove to a wire rack to cool completely. Slice as desired. The bread should be moist, not dry. Serves 10 to 12.

Chocolate Chunk Banana Bread

1 2/3 cups all-purpose flour
1 teaspoon baking soda
1/2 teaspoon salt
1/4 teaspoon cinnamon
1 cup plus 2 tablespoons sugar

2 eggs
1/2 cup vegetable oil
3 1/2 very ripe bananas, mashed
2 tablespoons crème fraîche or
    sour cream

1 teaspoon vanilla extract
1/2 cup walnuts or pecans, chopped
    (toasted if you prefer)
1/2 cup (3 ounces) chocolate
    chunks or chocolate chips

Preheat the oven to 350 degrees. Line the bottom of a loaf pan with baking parchment. Sift the flour, baking soda, salt and cinnamon together. Beat the sugar and eggs in the mixing bowl of a mixer fitted with a whisk attachment for 10 minutes or until light and fluffy. Drizzle in the oil, beating constantly until blended. Add the bananas, crème fraîche and vanilla and mix well. Fold in the dry ingredients, walnuts and chocolate chunks. Pour the batter into the prepared pan. Bake for 45 to 60 minutes or until the edges pull from the sides of the pan. Cool in the pan for 10 minutes. Remove to a wire rack to cool completely. Serves 6 to 10.

Photograph for these recipes on facing page.

Pear Preserve Bread

2 cups all-purpose flour
1 1/2 cups sugar
1 teaspoon baking soda
1 teaspoon salt

1 teaspoon nutmeg
1 teaspoon cinnamon
1 teaspoon ground allspice
1/2 teaspoon ground cloves
1 cup vegetable oil

3 eggs
1 cup buttermilk
1 tablespoon vanilla extract
1 pint good-quality pear preserves
1 cup chopped nuts

Preheat the oven to 350 degrees. Combine the flour, sugar, baking soda, salt, nutmeg, cinnamon, allspice and cloves in a mixing bowl and mix well. Add the oil and beat until blended. Add the eggs one at a time, beating well after each addition. Mix in the buttermilk and vanilla. Add the preserves and nuts and mix well. Pour the batter evenly into two greased loaf pans. Bake for 1 hour or until a wooden pick inserted in the center comes out clean. Cool in the pans for 10 minutes. Remove to a wire rack to cool completely. Serves 6 to 10.

Photograph for this recipe on page 27.

Pumpkin Butterscotch Muffins

1 3/4 cups all-purpose flour, sifted
1/2 cup packed light brown sugar
1/2 cup granulated sugar
1 teaspoon baking powder
1 teaspoon cinnamon

1/2 teaspoon ginger
1/2 teaspoon mace
1/4 teaspoon baking soda
1/4 teaspoon salt
1/8 teaspoon ground cloves
1 cup canned pumpkin

1/2 cup (1 stick) butter, melted
2 eggs
1 cup (6 ounces) butterscotch chips
1/4 cup chopped pecans, toasted
   (optional)

Preheat the oven to 350 degrees. Combine the flour, brown sugar, granulated sugar, baking powder, cinnamon, ginger, mace, baking soda, salt and cloves in a large bowl and mix well. Make a well in the center of the flour mixture.

Whisk the pumpkin, butter and eggs in a bowl until combined. Stir in the butterscotch chips and pecans. Add the pumpkin mixture to the well and fold just until the batter is moistened; do not overmix. Spoon the batter into greased muffin cups. Bake for 20 to 25 minutes or until a wooden pick inserted in the centers comes out clean. Cool in the pan for 2 minutes. Remove to a wire rack. Makes 2 dozen muffins.

Morning Glory Muffins

2 cups all-purpose flour
2 teaspoons baking soda
2 teaspoons cinnamon
1/2 teaspoon salt
1 1/4 cups sugar

1 cup vegetable oil
3 eggs, lightly beaten
2 teaspoons vanilla extract
2 cups grated carrots

1 Granny Smith apple, peeled
   and chopped
1/2 cup raisins
1/2 cup shredded coconut
1/2 cup chopped pecans

Preheat the oven to 350 degrees. Mix the flour, baking soda, cinnamon and salt together. Combine the sugar, oil, eggs, vanilla, carrots, apple, raisins, coconut and pecans in a bowl and mix well. Add the flour mixture and mix just until moistened.

Fill greased and floured or paper-lined muffin cups two-thirds full. Bake for 15 to 20 minutes or until the muffins test done. Cool in the pan for 2 minutes. Remove to a wire rack. Makes 2 dozen muffins.

Easy Overnight Cinnamon Rolls

3/4 cup packed brown sugar
1 cup (2 sticks) butter
1/2 cup chopped pecans

1 cup granulated sugar
1 tablespoon cinnamon
24 frozen dinner yeast rolls

1 (4-ounce) package butterscotch
   pudding and pie filling mix
1/2 cup chopped pecans

This recipe requires 8 hours rising time. Preheat the oven to 350 degrees. Combine the brown sugar and 1/2 cup of the butter in a saucepan. Cook over medium-low heat just until the brown sugar dissolves or until the mixture is no longer gritty. Pour over the bottom of a 9×13-inch baking pan, tilting the pan to coat evenly. Sprinkle with 1/2 cup pecans.

Combine the remaining 1/2 cup butter, the granulated sugar and cinnamon in a saucepan and cook until the butter melts. Lightly coat the frozen rolls with a portion of the butter mixture. Arrange the coated rolls over the prepared layer. Sprinkle with the pudding mix and 1/2 cup pecans and drizzle with any remaining butter mixture.

Loosely cover the rolls with greased foil. Place a tea towel over the foil to prevent the rolls from rising over the sides of the pan. Let rise for 8 to 10 hours. Bake, uncovered, for 25 to 30 minutes or until brown and bubbly. Let stand in the pan for 10 to 12 minutes; invert onto a serving platter. Makes 2 dozen rolls.

Family Favorite Cinnamon Rolls

Cinnamon Rolls

2 envelopes dry yeast

1/3 cup warm water (110 degrees)

1 2/3 cup warm milk (110 degrees)

3 tablespoons shortening

1/4 cup granulated sugar

2 teaspoons salt

5 cups all-purpose flour

1/4 cup water

3 tablespoons cinnamon

1 1/2 cups packed light brown sugar

1/2 cup (1 stick) butter, softened

1 1/2 cups raisins

1 1/2 cups chopped pecans

Gooey Spread

2 cups packed light brown sugar

1 cup (2 sticks) butter, softened

1/2 cup light corn syrup

2 tablespoons water

1/4 cup water

Confectioners' Sugar Icing
(see sidebar)

Confectioners' Sugar Icing

Combine 1 cup confectioners' sugar, 1/4 cup (1/2 stick) butter, 1 tablespoon (or more) milk and 1/4 teaspoon vanilla in a bowl and stir until of a drizzling consistency, adding additional milk as needed.

*T*his recipe requires 1 hour and 40 minutes rising time. Preheat the oven to 325 degrees. Read the recipe carefully before proceeding as there are two options.

For the cinnamon rolls, dissolve the yeast in the warm water in a bowl. Mix the warm milk, shortening, granulated sugar and salt in a large bowl. Stir in the yeast mixture. Add the flour 1 cup at a time, mixing until combined after each addition with a wooden spoon; a soft dough should form. Knead the dough with greased hands on a lightly floured surface for 1 minute or until a smooth ball forms. Place the dough in a greased bowl, turning to coat the surface. Lightly cover the bowl. Place the bowl in the kitchen sink and add enough warm water to the sink to reach 3 to 4 inches up the side of the bowl. Let rise for 30 to 40 minutes or until doubled in bulk. Combine 1/4 cup water and the cinnamon in a bowl and stir until of a paste consistency. Add the brown sugar and butter and stir until smooth. Divide the dough into two equal portions on a lightly floured surface. Cover one of the portions with a tea towel. Roll the remaining portion into a 12×16-inch rectangle. Spread half the cinnamon mixture over the rectangle and sprinkle with half the raisins and half the pecans. Roll to enclose the filling, pinching the seam to seal. Cut into 1 1/2-inch slices. Repeat the process with the remaining ingredients.

For the gooey spread, combine the brown sugar, butter, corn syrup and 2 tablespoons water in a bowl and stir until smooth. Spread half the brown sugar mixture over the bottom of a greased 9×13-inch baking pan. Arrange the rolls in a single layer on top. Spread the remaining brown sugar mixture over the top. Let rise for 30 minutes. Sprinkle with 1/4 cup water. Place the pan on the middle oven rack with a sheet of foil below the pan to catch any drippings. Bake for 12 minutes; gently press the rolls down with a metal spatula. Bake for 18 to 20 minutes longer or until brown and bubbly. Cool slightly in the pan on a wire rack. Serve warm directly from the baking pan or invert onto a baking sheet.

For cinnamon rolls with icing, omit the gooey spread and bake as directed above. Drizzle Confectioners' Sugar Icing (at left) over the warm rolls. Let stand for several minutes before serving. Serve warm. Makes 12 to 16 rolls.

Photograph for this recipe on facing page.

Cherry Almond Scones

3¼ cups all-purpose flour
¾ cup sugar
2 tablespoons baking powder
1 teaspoon salt

1½ cups (3 sticks) butter, chilled
    and cut into small pieces
¾ cup heavy whipping cream
¼ cup milk
1 tablespoon good-quality
    almond extract

¼ cup dried cherries
¾ cup almonds, blanched
    and sliced
1 egg, beaten
Sliced almonds to taste

*T*his recipe requires 1 hour of refrigeration. Preheat the oven to 375 degrees. Mix the flour, sugar, baking powder and salt in a bowl. Cut the butter into the flour mixture using a pastry blender until the consistency of coarse meal. Add the cream, milk, flavoring and cherries and mix until a dough forms. Gently mix in ¾ cup almonds.

Divide the dough into two equal portions. Roll or pat each portion into a 1-inch-thick round on a lightly floured surface. Cut each round into six to eight wedges.

Arrange the wedges on a baking sheet lined with baking parchment. Brush the tops with the egg using a pastry brush. Sprinkle with sliced almonds to taste and gently press to adhere. Or, you can sprinkle with coarse sugar. Chill, covered, for at least 1 hour or overnight. You may freeze at this point for future use. Bake for 20 to 30 minutes or until golden brown. Cool on the baking sheet for 2 minutes. Remove to a wire rack. Store in an airtight container. Makes 12 to 16 scones.

*M*y fondest memory around our kitchen table growing up was the celebration of a "Birthday Breakfast." My mom would always set our round, oak table with her fine china, silver, and crystal and serve us a delicious breakfast on the morning of our birthday. We would unwrap gifts and sing "Happy Birthday." I inherited that same oak table and have continued the "Birthday Breakfast" tradition with my own children and husband. The table was originally from my great-grandmother's home in North Texas, and my grandmother shared with me that the base of the table was built from one oak tree over 75 years ago.   —S. Mills

Honey Puff

3 ounces cream cheese, cubed
   and softened
1 cup all-purpose flour
1 cup milk

6 eggs
3 tablespoons honey
1 teaspoon vanilla extract
1/2 teaspoon salt

1/2 teaspoon baking powder
3 tablespoons butter
2 tablespoons confectioners' sugar
Fresh seasonal fruit (optional)

Preheat the oven to 375 degrees. Combine the cream cheese, flour, milk, eggs, honey, vanilla, salt and baking powder in a blender. Process on High for 2 to 4 minutes or until blended.

Heat the butter in a 10-inch ovenproof skillet or baking pan in the oven until melted. Pour the cream cheese mixture into the prepared skillet. Bake for 25 to 30 minutes or until a knife inserted in the center comes out clean. Sprinkle with confectioners' sugar. Garnish with fruit. The puff will rise and fall like a soufflé. Serves 6.

This recipe is from the League's first publication, Texas Ties. For order information on this publication or our most recent publication, Texas Tables, contact the League at 888.TEX.TIES.

A couple of years after my husband and I moved into our first home in South Texas, we got tired of sitting around the house on our own watching parades and football all by ourselves on New Year's Day. So, the next year we invited a few of our neighbors over for a very casual open house on New Year's Day. We laid out a spread of food in the kitchen, turned on the television in the living room, and spread out the first newspaper of the New Year on the dining room table. Our gatherings were so casual, neighbors would wander over with empty coffee cups. People would migrate from one room to another . . . get food and drink in the kitchen, eat and converse in the dining room, move into the living room to watch TV . . . repeat. A couple of years later, we began to invite friends we saw during the holiday season as well as our neighbors. The table became a place where friends from the different parts of our lives would meet and create their own new friendships. Because my husband and I were both removed from our own families during the holiday season, the brunch was a great way to begin the New Year with the reminder that we were blessed to have a second family of close and loving friends.   —P. Chandler

The Picnic Table

Step into the light side of meals with delicious recipes of soups, salads, and sandwiches, all great for relaxing summertime picnics, but also perfectly suited for the busiest of lifestyles. Once thought of as only a course prior to more substantial food to come, today's soups and salads, much varied and artfully crafted, easily serve as the main fare.

Soups, served elegantly in a tea cup or cooked over a campfire, are lovingly gifted to those ready to be fulfilled and comforted. Salads are especially popular in our warm climate, where it can often be too hot to eat anything else. No food option is better "on-the-go" than sandwiches. Sandwiches of all varieties are staples for backyard picnics and made all the more special by sharing them on the run to family activities, lending a twist to the modernized table traditions and proving that where you eat is not as important as with whom you eat.

> *"To make a good salad is to be a brilliant diplomatist—*
> *the problem is entirely the same in both cases.*
> *To know how much oil one must mix with one's vinegar."*
>
> —Oscar Wilde

Rodeo Chili

1/3 cup vegetable shortening
1 pound beef chuck,
    cut into chunks
1 white onion, chopped
2 ribs celery, finely chopped
2 large garlic cloves, chopped
1 green bell pepper, roasted
    and chopped
2 jalapeño peppers, roasted, seeded
    and chopped
1 poblano pepper, roasted, seeded
    and chopped

1 (6-ounce) can tomato paste
1 (28-ounce) can Italian
    plum tomatoes
3 (10-ounce) cans diced tomatoes
    with green chiles
2 cups chicken stock
1/2 (12-ounce) bottle favorite
    dark beer
1/3 cup dry red wine
2 tablespoons dark chili powder
    (New Mexico red chili
    powder preferred)

1 1/2 teaspoons Mexican oregano
1 1/2 teaspoons ground cumin
1 1/2 teaspoons coriander
1 teaspoon whole cumin seeds
1 (16-ounce) can pinto beans
1 (16-ounce) can black beans
Sea salt to taste
Cracked pepper to taste
Shredded Colby cheese (optional)
Coarsely chopped fresh cilantro
    (optional)

Melt the shortening in a stockpot and add the beef. Cook until the beef is brown on all sides. Stir in the onion, celery and garlic and sauté until the vegetables are tender. Add the bell pepper, jalapeño peppers, poblano pepper and tomato paste and mix well.

Cook until the tomato paste turns dark in color, stirring occasionally. Chop the plum tomatoes, reserving the juices. Add the tomatoes and reserved tomato juice to the stockpot. Stir in the tomatoes with green chiles, stock, beer, wine, chili powder, oregano, ground cumin, coriander and cumin seeds. Bring to a boil; reduce the heat.

Simmer for about 1 1/2 to 2 hours. Add the undrained beans, salt and pepper and simmer for 30 minutes. Ladle into chili bowls and top with cheese and cilantro. Serves 10.

Smoky Enchilada Soup

1 can chipotle peppers in adobo
    sauce
1/4 cup vegetable oil
1 1/2 cups finely chopped onions
2 tablespoons chicken base
1 or 2 garlic cloves, chopped
1 to 2 teaspoons salt
1 teaspoon ground cumin

1 teaspoon chili powder
1/2 teaspoon black pepper
1/4 teaspoon cayenne pepper
8 cups water
1 cup masa harina
1 cup crushed tomatoes
4 ounces processed American
    cheese, cubed

1 1/2 pounds chicken, cooked
    and chopped
2 tablespoons chopped cilantro
8 ounces queso fresco, crumbled
    (optional)

Drain the chipotle peppers, reserving 1 tablespoon of the adobo sauce. Chop one pepper. Heat the oil in a stockpot or Dutch oven and add the onions, chopped chipotle pepper, reserved adobo sauce, chicken base and garlic and mix well. Stir in the salt, cumin, chili powder, black pepper and cayenne pepper. Sauté until the onions are tender.

Mix 2 cups of the water and the masa harina in a measuring cup until smooth; stir into the onion mixture. Cook for about 5 minutes, stirring constantly. Add the remaining water and the tomatoes and bring to a boil. Cook until of the desired consistency, stirring occasionally.

Reduce the heat and stir in the American cheese. Simmer until the cheese melts, stirring occasionally. Mix in the chicken and cilantro. Ladle into soup bowls and garnish with the queso fresco. Serves 6 to 8.

As a child, our paint-chipped, tile-topped, factory-assembled kitchen/dining room table was always covered with a tablecloth reflecting the season. Mom believed that dressing the table made things better, given the disheveled look of our modest-size table with shaky legs and mismatched yellow vinyl chairs. Discussions and debates livened up the table as if we were policymakers on the cusp of changing the world over vegetable soup. The table provided a revolving door to new faces and foods that made unexpected appearances throughout the years. Even when there was absolutely no room to squeeze in a mouse, real estate magically appeared and we could all resume eating again. Today, as a new parent, my hope is that our kitchen table becomes a place of comfort, excitement, and joy for my family and those who pass through the front door. —E. White

Hot Lime Tortilla Soup

12 cups chicken stock
1 bunch cilantro
1 large jalapeño pepper, seeded and
    cut lengthwise into strips
1 onion, finely chopped
1 green bell pepper, finely chopped
1 garlic clove, minced
1 to 2 tablespoons vegetable oil

2 large tomatoes, seeded
    and chopped
1 onion, coarsely chopped
2 banana peppers, seeded and
    sliced crosswise
1 poblano pepper, seeded and
    coarsely chopped
2 chicken bouillon cubes

2 boneless skinless chicken breasts,
    poached and shredded
1 jar pimentos, finely chopped
1/2 teaspoon salt
5 tablespoons fresh lime juice
8 corn tortillas, cut into strips and
    lightly fried
2 or 3 limes, thinly sliced

Bring the stock to a boil in a stockpot. Reserve several sprigs of the cilantro for garnish and add the remaining cilantro and the jalapeño pepper to the stockpot. Boil for 5 minutes. Remove from the heat and cool slightly.

Sauté the finely chopped onion, bell pepper and garlic in the oil in a skillet. Do not overcook. Stir in the tomatoes and cook over medium heat for 5 minutes. Strain the stock of the cilantro and jalapeño pepper. Add the cooked tomato mixture, coarsely chopped onion, all the peppers, the bouillon cubes and shredded chicken. Simmer for 25 to 30 minutes. Stir in the pimentos, salt and lime juice.

Line soup bowls with some of the tortilla strips and place a lime slice in the bottom of each bowl. Ladle the soup into the prepared bowls. Garnish each serving with the reserved cilantro and the remaining tortilla strips. Serves 12 to 15.

Lobster Bisque

1/2 cup extra-virgin olive oil
8 ounces each carrots, celery and
    onions, cut into 1-inch pieces
1/4 cup chopped shallots

4 whole Maine lobsters
8 cups water
1/2 (750-milliliter) bottle sherry
1/2 (750-milliliter) bottle madeira

1 cup white rice or arborio rice
1/2 cup tomato paste
1/4 cup heavy whipping cream
Salt and pepper to taste

Heat the olive oil in a large stockpot and add the carrots, celery, onions and shallots. Cook over medium heat for 15 minutes. Add the lobsters and sauté for 8 to 10 minutes. Stir in the water, sherry and madeira. Bring to a boil. Reduce the heat and simmer for 45 to 60 minutes. Add the rice and tomato paste and bring to a boil. Boil until thickened. Remove the lobsters to a platter. Remove the meat from the lobster tails and claws. Strain the bisque and return to the stockpot, discarding the solids. Stir the lobster meat and cream into the strained bisque and season with salt and pepper. Do not reheat. Ladle into soup bowls. May use four lobster tails instead of whole lobsters. Serves 4.

Courtesy of Sorrento Ristorante

Soupe à l'Oignon Gratinée

2 thick slices bacon, julienned
2 to 3 tablespoons butter
3 garlic cloves, sliced
4 cups thinly sliced onions
1/2 cup white wine
4 cups chicken stock

4 cups beef stock
3 cups water
1 bay leaf
1 tablespoon chopped fresh
    thyme leaves
1 tablespoon salt

1 1/2 teaspoons pepper
1 loaf French bread, thinly sliced
1 cup (4 ounces) grated Swiss
    cheese or Gruyère cheese

Preheat the oven to the broiler setting. Render the bacon in the butter in a stockpot. Add the garlic and cook until the garlic is light brown. Add 1 cup of the onions and cook until the onions are light brown, stirring constantly. Deglaze the stockpot with the wine. Add the remaining onions, the chicken stock, beef stock and the desired amount of water and mix well. Add the bay leaf. Cook for 1 hour, stirring occasionally. Add the thyme, salt and pepper and cook for 3 hours or until the onions are very tender. Discard the bay leaf. Ladle the soup into ovenproof soup bowls and arrange the bowls on a baking sheet. Top each serving with a slice of bread and sprinkle with the cheese. Broil until brown. Serve immediately. Serves 12.

Creamy Asparagus Soup

1 1/2 pounds asparagus
1/4 cup (1/2 stick) butter
1 cup chopped yellow onion
1/2 cup chopped celery

2 tablespoons minced garlic
1/4 cup dry white wine
1 to 3 tablespoons
   all-purpose flour
4 cups chicken broth

1 to 2 teaspoons salt
1/2 teaspoon freshly cracked
   black pepper
1/4 teaspoon cayenne pepper
2 cups heavy whipping cream

Snap off the thick woody ends of the asparagus spears and discard. Chop the asparagus. Reserve half of the asparagus tips for garnish. Blanch the reserved asparagus tips in boiling water in a saucepan; drain.

Melt the butter in a sauté pan and add the onion and celery. Sauté until the onion is almost translucent. Add the remaining asparagus and the garlic. Sauté until the asparagus is tender. Stir in the wine and cook until most of the wine has evaporated. Add enough of the flour to make a roux and mix well. Cook for about 5 minutes, stirring frequently. Gradually whisk in the broth, salt, black pepper and cayenne pepper. Bring to a boil; reduce the heat.

Simmer for about 20 minutes and stir in the cream. Return to a boil; immediately reduce the heat. Simmer for 10 minutes. Purée the soup in batches in a blender or food processor. Strain through a sieve into the saucepan, discarding the solids. Taste and adjust the seasonings. Ladle into cups or soup bowls and garnish with the reserved blanched asparagus spears. Serves 8.

Photograph for this recipe on facing page.

The dining room is my personal space in our home. With a blended family of four teenage and adult-age children, we are typical of today's on-the-go family, and living in our home is very casual. The rest of the house usually takes on a "lived-in" look, but not my dining room. No matter what condition the rest of the house may be in, my dining room is pristine and lovely to behold. It's a beautiful room with dark red walls, hardwood floors, crown moulding, and a four-foot-wide arched window fitted with beautiful shutters. It contains a custom-built dining room table and chairs and decorating elements personally selected by me. The function of my dining room is as most, hosting holiday dinners, special family occasions, and bunco—but for me it means more. My dining room is my lovely oasis of calm and order, a place not only to celebrate the special occasions of life, but also a place for me to relax and catch my breath in the storm of everyday living.   —D. Silver

Butternut Squash Soup

1 (1½-pound) butternut squash
Vegetable oil
1 cup chicken stock
½ cup finely chopped andouille
    sausage
¼ cup chopped onion
1 teaspoon minced garlic

1 tablespoon vegetable oil
1 teaspoon hot pepper sauce
1 teaspoon Worcestershire sauce
Dash of nutmeg
Creole seasoning to taste
2 cups chicken stock
Salt and pepper to taste

Brown sugar (optional)
12 (¼-inch) slices andouille
    sausage, cut into half-moons
1 Granny Smith apple, peeled
    and chopped

Cutting Butternut Squash

Using a large chef's knife, slice a small piece off each end of the squash to create flat surfaces. Cut the squash in half, separating the narrow and bulbous ends. Stand the slender piece on one flat end and remove the tough outer peel by slicing from top to bottom. For the rounded piece, use a vegetable peeler to pare off the skin. Cut that section in half and then remove the seeds with a metal spoon. Cut the squash into ½-inch chunks.

Preheat the oven to 350 degrees. Cut the squash lengthwise into halves and remove the seeds. Brush the cut sides of the squash lightly with oil and arrange the squash cut side down in a baking pan. Roast for 45 to 60 minutes or until the squash is tender. Scoop out enough of the squash to measure 4 cups. Process 4 cups squash with 1 cup stock in a blender until puréed.

Sauté the chopped sausage, onion and garlic in 1 tablespoon oil in a large saucepan until the onion is tender. Stir in the puréed squash mixture, hot sauce, Worcestershire sauce, nutmeg, Creole seasoning and 2 cups stock. Strain the soup at this point for a finer consistency, if desired. Bring to a boil; reduce the heat.

Simmer for 10 to 15 minutes. Season with salt and pepper. Taste for flavor and consistency. If a sweeter taste is desired, add a small amount of brown sugar. If the soup is too thin, cook until reduced to the desired consistency or add additional puréed squash. You may chill, covered, for future use at this point.

Render the sliced sausage in a small amount of oil in a small skillet over medium heat just until the sausage begins to brown. Add the apple and sauté just until the apple is tender. Ladle the soup into bowls and garnish with the apple and sausage mixture. Serves 6.

Courtesy of Carl Walker, Executive Chef, Brennan's of Houston

Southwest Potato and Leek Soup

3 tablespoons butter
3 leek bulbs, chopped
    (about 2 1/2 cups)
3 garlic cloves, chopped
8 cups chopped peeled Idaho
    baking potatoes
4 cups chicken broth
2 cups milk

1 cup heavy cream
1 (7-ounce) can chopped
    green chiles
1 teaspoon salt
1/2 cup sour cream
1/4 cup heavy cream
1/2 cup hot red taco sauce
2 green onions, chopped (optional)

*M*elt the butter in a large saucepan and add the leeks and garlic. Sauté for 5 minutes. Stir in the potatoes and broth and bring to a boil. Reduce the heat.

Simmer, covered, for 30 minutes or until the potatoes are tender. Add the milk, 1 cup cream, the green chiles and salt and mix well. Bring to a simmer and simmer for 5 minutes. Purée the soup using a handheld immersion blender or process in batches in a blender.

Combine the sour cream, 1/4 cup heavy cream and the taco sauce in a food processor and process until combined. Ladle the soup into bowls and swirl some of the sour cream mixture into each serving. Garnish with the green onions.

For baked potato soup, omit the sour cream mixture and garnish the soup with crumbled crisp-cooked bacon, sour cream, shredded Cheddar cheese and chopped green onions. Serves 4.

*O*ur first Christmas as a married couple, my husband and I shared a meal on a blanket next to our tree after we finished trimming it. It was so special and beautiful to us, that we continued the tradition every year. Though we have missed spending time around the holiday table with our families at the holidays, the warm glow of the twinkle lights and sparkling ornaments make our romantic picnic a perfect time to reflect on our own growing family. —K. Sanders

Creamy Tomato Basil Soup

2 tablespoons olive oil
1 cup coarsely chopped onion
1/2 cup coarsely chopped celery
3 garlic cloves, crushed

6 cups chopped tomatoes
4 cups tomato juice or vegetable
   juice cocktail
16 fresh basil leaves
1 cup whipping cream

1/2 cup (1 stick) unsalted
   butter, cubed
1 teaspoon salt
1/4 teaspoon cracked pepper
Basil leaves (optional)

Heat a large saucepan and pour in the olive oil. Sauté the onion, celery and garlic in the hot oil until the onion and celery are tender. Add the tomatoes and tomato juice and mix well. Simmer over medium-low heat for 30 minutes. Cool slightly.

Process the tomato mixture and sixteen basil leaves in a blender or food processor until puréed. Strain into the saucepan, discarding the solids. Add the cream and butter.

Simmer over low heat until the cream and butter are incorporated, stirring frequently. Stir in the salt and pepper. Ladle into soups bowls and garnish with additional basil leaves. Serve with crusty bread. Serves 8.

Photograph for this recipe on page 34.

My Junior League Table is full and overflowing to the brim. Interwoven into my tabletop are memories from more than twelve years of service in three Leagues in Texas. My Junior League Table memories start off with the Provisional Table, which is filled with wonderful memories of friendships made along the way with training to assist the community and develop leadership skills. My Active Table relishes memories of community programs, Holiday Market planning, and meals served around a table or even a kitchen bar while planning activities for the upcoming year. From casual sandwiches to elegant "Texas" fare, the Community Table is filled with passion to create programs that assist our communities and fund-raisers that help support these programs. My Board Table memories include a table filled with agendas, calendars, time lines, and management connected with food to share from a member's favorite appetizer recipe to a birthday cake celebrating a board member's birthday. Each member landed at the Board Table after a day filled with work and family activities and also made time for assisting the League in maintaining a strong foundation for our members and community. My Junior League Table is a very long table covering a hilltop for miles and miles, making room for all of my League friends and their families. The table has beautiful white linens and food crafted with heart and soul. This is truly my "Texas Table." —A. May

Roasted Poblano and Corn Chowder

Chowder
6 ears corn with husks
1 poblano pepper
2 tablespoons butter
1 onion, finely chopped
1 tablespoon minced garlic
2 cups dry white wine
5 cups chicken broth

1 cup heavy whipping cream
1 to 2 tablespoons cilantro, chopped
1 teaspoon salt
1 teaspoon freshly cracked pepper

Chipotle Cream
1/2 cup sour cream

2 teaspoons canned chipotle
   peppers, puréed
1 teaspoon fresh lime juice
Pinch of salt
Pinch of pepper
Chopped fresh cilantro (optional)

*P*reheat the oven to 375 degrees.

For the chowder, roast the corn in the oven for 45 minutes. Let stand until cool. Remove the husks and silk. Cut the kernels from the cobs into a bowl using a sharp knife. If the fresh corn is light in color, substitute 1 1/2 cups frozen corn for three of the fresh ears for a more intense yellow chowder.

Roast the poblano pepper directly over an open flame on a gas cooktop or grill until charred on all sides, turning frequently. Place in a sealable plastic bag and seal tightly. Let stand until cool. Rinse under cold water to remove the skin, seeds and stem; chop the poblano pepper.

Melt the butter in a large stockpot. Add the onion and garlic and sauté until the onion is tender. Stir in the wine. Cook for 10 to 15 minutes or until the mixture is the consistency of a thick syrup, stirring occasionally. Mix in the corn and cook for 5 minutes. Add the broth and bring to a boil. Reduce the heat.

Simmer for 20 to 30 minutes. Add the cream and bring to a boil. Immediately reduce the heat and cook until the soup begins to thicken, stirring frequently. Stir in the poblano pepper. Let stand until cool. Process the soup in batches in a food processor until puréed. Return the purée to the stockpot and stir in the cilantro, salt and pepper. Simmer just until heated through.

For the cream, combine the sour cream, chipotle peppers, lime juice, salt and pepper in a bowl and mix well. Spoon the cream into a squeeze bottle or sealable plastic bag with one corner removed. To serve, ladle the warm soup into soup bowls and top with a dollop of the cream. Garnish with cilantro. Serves 10.

Chipotle Sweet Potato Soup

1 tablespoon unsalted butter
1 1/2 cups chopped white onions
2 tablespoons brown sugar
1 teaspoon salt
1/2 teaspoon cinnamon

1 garlic clove, minced
6 cups chopped peeled
   sweet potatoes
2 chipotle peppers in adobo
   sauce, chopped

5 cups low-sodium chicken stock
1 cup half-and-half
3 tablespoons lime juice
Sour cream (optional)
Chopped chives (optional)

Melt the butter in a stockpot over medium-high heat. Add the onions, brown sugar, salt and cinnamon. Sauté for 4 minutes or until the onions are light brown. Stir in the garlic and sauté for 1 minute. Add the sweet potatoes and chipotle peppers and mix well.

Sauté for 10 minutes. Stir in the stock and bring to a boil. Reduce the heat and simmer for 25 minutes or until the sweet potatoes are tender, stirring occasionally.

Remove from the heat and cool for 10 minutes or longer. Pour half the soup into a blender and process until smooth. Repeat the process with the remaining soup. Pour both batches of the puréed soup into the stockpot.

Pour the half-and-half into a microwave-safe bowl. Microwave on High for about 1 minute or until heated through. Stir the warm half-and-half and lime juice into the soup. Ladle in soup bowls and garnish with a dollop of sour cream and chives. You may chill, covered, for future use. Reheat before serving. If you are unable to tolerate the heat from two chipotle chiles, cut the amount in half. Serves 6.

Photograph for this recipe on facing page.

Avocado Steak Salad

2 pounds beef tenderloin
1 teaspoon salt
1 teaspoon pepper
1 tablespoon butter

1 red onion, cut into thick slices
    and separated into rings
1/2 cup vegetable oil
1/2 cup wine vinegar
1/4 cup olive oil
2 teaspoons Dijon mustard

1 teaspoon salt
1 teaspoon pepper
1/3 bunch flat-leaf
    parsley, chopped
12 cups torn mixed greens
2 avocados, chopped

This recipe requires 8 hours of refrigeration. Preheat the oven to 350 degrees. Season the beef with 1 teaspoon salt and 1 teaspoon pepper. Arrange the beef in a roasting pan sprayed with nonstick cooking spray. Rub the surface of the beef with the butter. Bake for 30 minutes or until medium-rare. Or, sear in a cast-iron skillet over medium-high heat for 4 minutes per side. Let rest for 20 to 30 minutes before slicing. Slice the beef as desired.

Layer the beef and onion in a dish until all of the ingredients are used. Whisk the vegetable oil, vinegar, olive oil, Dijon mustard, 1 teaspoon salt, 1 teaspoon pepper and the parsley in a bowl until combined. Pour half the dressing over the prepared layer.

Marinate, covered, in the refrigerator for 8 to 10 hours. Mound 2 cups of the lettuce on each of six serving plates and top evenly with the beef mixture. Sprinkle evenly with the avocado. Drizzle with the remaining dressing. A great way to use leftover beef tenderloin. Serves 6.

Photograph for this recipe on facing page.

Japanese Chicken Salad

Asian Vinaigrette
2/3 cup olive oil
2 tablespoons sugar
1/2 cup rice wine vinegar
1 teaspoon salt

1/2 teaspoon pepper
1/4 teaspoon ground ginger

Chicken Salad
4 cups torn butter lettuce and
   red leaf lettuce
3 green onions, sliced

1/3 cup slivered almonds,
   lightly toasted
2 tablespoons sesame seeds, toasted
2 cups chopped cooked chicken
1 (11-ounce) can mandarin
   oranges, drained

For the vinaigrette, combine the olive oil, sugar, rice wine vinegar, salt, pepper and ginger in a jar with a tight-fitting lid and seal tightly. Shake to combine. Chill in the refrigerator.

For the salad, toss the lettuce, green onions, almonds and sesame seeds in a salad bowl. Mix in the chicken and mandarin oranges. Add the vinaigrette just before serving to prevent the lettuce from wilting. Serves 4 to 6.

My grandmother was a real character—even somewhat of a curmudgeon. She was pretty legendary in the little community where she lived. She was no-nonsense, but she was also a bit of a pill. And I loved her enormously! She didn't bake cookies or any of that sort of thing. In fact, she generally wasn't much of a cook. But she did have a way with seafood, especially her gumbo. She was famous for it!

I remember the great big family get-togethers at holiday time. She lived in this long, ranch-style house. You could walk straight through from the sunroom, to the breakfast room, to the dining room, and all the way through to the living room. During holidays she would line up tables that stretched nearly that entire distance. And those tables were piled high with every type of seafood dish imaginable—shrimp creole, étouffée, fried oysters, crabs, and shrimp gumbo. I especially loved the gumbo. Through the years, I have tried gumbo made by other people. It just isn't the same. It just doesn't measure up to the gumbo made by Dad and Grandma. There is always something missing. Maybe it's that little extra dash of love that they always made sure to include in the gumbo pot.
—G. Tonroy

Pesto Chicken Salad with Artichokes

Basil Pesto
4 garlic cloves
3 tablespoons pine nuts, toasted
1 teaspoon salt
1/4 teaspoon pepper
2 cups loosely packed basil
3/4 cup (3 ounces) grated
    Parmesan cheese
1/2 cup olive oil

Chicken Salad
1 1/2 pounds boneless skinless
    chicken breasts
Salt and pepper to taste
1 (14-ounce) can artichoke hearts,
    drained and chopped
1/4 cup finely chopped celery
1/4 cup finely chopped
    yellow onion

1/4 cup sour cream
1/4 cup mayonnaise
4 croissants or any type of bread
    (optional)

Preheat the oven to 350 degrees.

For the pesto, process the garlic, pine nuts, salt and pepper in a blender until puréed. Add the basil, cheese and olive oil and process to the desired consistency. Serve immediately or store in an airtight container in the refrigerator.

For the salad, coat the chicken with 1 to 2 ounces of the pesto or enough to cover. Season with salt and pepper. Arrange the chicken in a baking pan. Bake for 10 to 12 minutes or until cooked through. Let stand until cool; cut into bite-size pieces.

Toss the chicken, artichokes, celery and onion together in a salad bowl. Add the remaining pesto, the sour cream and mayonnaise and stir until coated. Season with salt and pepper. Serve in croissants for a nice presentation. Serves 4.

Photograph for this recipe on page 35.

Celery

Texas has an ideal climate and excellent growing conditions for the production of crisp, dark green celery with long stalks. A minor yet important Texas crop, celery is produced on between four hundred and five hundred acres. Texas produces twenty-six million pounds of this crunchy favorite that adds flavor and texture to winter salads each year.

Cilantro Lime Crab Salad in Avocado Halves

2 tomatoes, seeded and chopped
1/3 cup finely chopped red onion
2 tablespoons chopped
   fresh cilantro
1/2 teaspoon ground cumin
1/2 teaspoon grated lime zest
2 teaspoons fresh lime juice
3 tablespoons mayonnaise

8 ounces lump crab meat, drained
   and shells removed
Salt and pepper to taste
1 large ripe avocado, cut into halves
1 teaspoon fresh lime juice
Chopped fresh cilantro (optional)
1 lime, peeled and cut into wedges

Combine the tomatoes, onion, 2 tablespoons cilantro, the cumin, lime zest and 2 teaspoons lime juice in a bowl and mix well. Stir in the mayonnaise. Fold in the crab meat and season with salt and pepper.

Brush the cut sides of the avocado halves with 1 teaspoon lime juice to prevent discoloration. Mound equal portions of the crab meat salad in each avocado half and arrange each stuffed avocado half on a serving plate. Garnish with chopped cilantro. Arrange the lime wedges around the stuffed avocado halves. Serve immediately. Serves 2.

Photograph for this recipe on facing page.

Grape Salad

8 ounces cream cheese, softened
1/2 cup granulated sugar
1 cup sour cream
1 teaspoon vanilla extract
1 pound seedless red grapes,
   cut into halves

1 pound seedless green grapes,
   cut into halves
3/4 cup packed brown sugar
1/2 cup chopped pecans

*T*his recipe requires 8 hours of refrigeration. Beat the cream cheese and granulated sugar in a mixing bowl until creamy. Mix the sour cream and vanilla in a bowl. Add the sour cream mixture and grapes to the cream cheese mixture and mix until coated.

Spoon the grape salad into a crystal serving bowl. Sprinkle with the brown sugar and pecans. Chill, covered, for 8 to 10 hours. Serve chilled. Serves 12.

Tomatoes Vinaigrette

3 large red tomatoes
3 large yellow tomatoes
6 tablespoons minced
   flat-leaf parsley
6 tablespoons olive oil

2 tablespoons apple cider vinegar
1 garlic clove, minced
1 teaspoon salt
1/2 teaspoon dried basil
1/8 teaspoon pepper

*T*his recipe requires 8 hours of refrigeration. Blanch the tomatoes in boiling water in a saucepan to loosen the skins; drain. Remove the skins from the tomatoes and discard. Slice the tomatoes. Alternately arrange the red and yellow tomato slices slightly overlapping on a serving platter. Sprinkle with the parsley.

Combine the olive oil, vinegar, garlic, salt, basil and pepper in a jar with a tight-fitting lid and seal tightly. Shake to mix. Pour over the tomatoes. Chill, covered, for 8 to 10 hours. Serves 8 to 10.

Whole Wheat Pasta Salad with Walnuts and Feta Cheese

Walnut Vinaigrette
2 tablespoons walnut oil
2 tablespoons red wine vinegar
1 garlic clove, minced
1/2 teaspoon Dijon mustard

Whole Wheat Pasta Salad
8 ounces whole wheat fusilli or any whole wheat pasta
1/2 cup walnut pieces or halves
1 1/2 cups chopped baby spinach leaves

1/2 cup crumbled feta cheese
1/2 cup chopped white onion
2 tablespoons chopped red onion
Salt and pepper to taste

For the vinaigrette, whisk the walnut oil, vinegar, garlic and Dijon mustard in a bowl until combined.

For the salad, cook the pasta using the package directions; drain. Rinse with cold water and drain again. Place the pasta in a bowl and chill, covered, in the refrigerator. Toast the walnuts in a sauté pan over medium-high heat for about 2 minutes or until the walnuts are fragrant. Remove to a plate to cool. Coarsely chop the walnuts.

Toss the chilled pasta, walnuts, spinach, cheese, white onion and red onion in a bowl. Add the vinaigrette and toss until coated. Season with salt and pepper. Serves 6.

Tables, Tables, Tables . . . I love all the tables in our home! It is hard to decide which one is my favorite. Is it the round wooden kitchen table where we sit for everyday meals, do our homework, blow out birthday candles, and make gingerbread houses at Christmas time? Or is it the dining room table that was passed down to us by my husband's grandmother? Forever faithful, my dining table is decorated for EVERY holiday and holds many special memories of candlelight dinners, holiday meals, and dinner parties. Another favorite is the fragile checkerboard table. While we've always found the perfect place in every home for this little table, we never actually use it. But I triple-love this precious piece of furniture! Last but not least is my antique barley twist table. This old-timer, with its drop leaf, is the most multipurpose table in the house. We have used it as a sideboard, side table, craft table, eating table, desk, and much more. As you can see, I could never pick a favorite. I hope one day my daughters will treasure all my "Texas Tables" as much as I do! Bon appétit, ya'll.
—A. Henderson

Mixed Antipasto

Marinade

1 large garlic clove, minced

2 tablespoons balsamic vinegar

2 tablespoons red wine vinegar

1 teaspoon dried basil, crumbled

1 teaspoon dried
   oregano, crumbled

1/2 teaspoon dried
   rosemary, crumbled

1/4 teaspoon red pepper flakes,
   or to taste

Salt and pepper to taste

1/2 cup olive oil

Antipasto

3 large carrots, cut diagonally into
   1/4-inch slices

2 fennel bulbs, cut crosswise into
   1/4-inch slices (about 3 cups)

2 red bell peppers, roasted and
   cut into strips

2 yellow bell peppers, roasted and
   cut into strips

1 (12-ounce) jar pepperoncini,
   drained

12 ounces kalamata olives and/or
   green olives

4 ounces oil-pack sun-dried
   tomatoes, drained and
   cut into strips

12 ounces bocconcini (small
   mozzarella balls)

8 ounces pepperoni or sopressata,
   cut into 1/4-inch slices and
   cut into quarters

2 (7-ounce) jars marinated
   artichoke hearts, drained and
   cut into quarters

1/3 cup minced fresh
   flat-leaf parsley

Sprigs of parsley (optional)

This recipe requires 4 hours of refrigeration.

For the marinade, whisk the garlic, balsamic vinegar, wine vinegar, basil, oregano rosemary, red pepper flakes, salt and pepper in a bowl until combined. Add the olive oil gradually, whisking constantly until emulsified.

For the antipasto, blanch the carrots and fennel in boiling water in a saucepan for 3 to 4 minutes or until tender-crisp; drain. Immediately plunge the carrots and fennel into a bowl of ice water to stop the cooking process; drain.

Toss the carrots, fennel, bell peppers, pepperoncini, olives, sun-dried tomatoes, bocconcini, pepperoni, artichokes, minced parsley and marinade together in a large bowl until coated. Chill, covered, for 4 to 10 hours, stirring occasionally. Arrange the antipasto on a serving platter. Garnish with sprigs of parsley. Serve at room temperature. Serve as an appetizer, side dish or entrée over cooked cavatappi pasta. Serves 6 to 8.

Caesar Salad

Croutons
1 garlic clove
1/3 cup (or more) olive oil
2 cups (1/2-inch) cubes crusty
    French bread
Kosher salt to taste
Freshly ground pepper to taste

Caesar Salad
1 head romaine
Salt to taste
1 teaspoon olive oil
1 garlic clove
1 large anchovy
1/4 teaspoon dry mustard
1 teaspoon red wine vinegar

1 teaspoon Worcestershire sauce
Juice of 1/2 lemon
2 teaspoons olive oil
1 egg yolk with small amount of
    egg white
3 to 4 teaspoons grated
    Parmesan cheese
Freshly ground pepper to taste

*P*reheat the oven to 350 degrees.

For the croutons, mash the garlic clove with the olive oil in a bowl. Lightly brush the bread cubes with the garlic mixture, adding additional olive oil as needed. Sprinkle with salt and pepper. Arrange the bread cubes in a single layer on a baking sheet. Bake for 15 minutes or until golden brown, turning occasionally. Remove to a plate to cool.

For the salad, separate the romaine into leaves and rinse. Pat the leaves dry and tear into bite-size pieces. Keep the romaine covered by a napkin to ensure it will be dry when ready to add to the salad.

Sprinkle a small amount of salt in a large wooden bowl and add 1 teaspoon olive oil. Pierce the garlic clove with a fork and swirl the garlic clove in the olive oil mixture, coating the side of the bowl with the olive oil and juice of the garlic. Smash the garlic clove and mix with the olive oil mixture until a smooth paste forms. Add the anchovy and smash with the fork until blended with the garlic mixture. Add the dry mustard, vinegar, Worcestershire sauce and lemon juice and mix well. Add 2 teaspoons olive oil and the egg yolk with a small amount of egg white. Mix until the mixture is creamy and smooth. Stir in 1 teaspoon of the cheese.

Add the romaine and toss until all the dressing adheres to the romaine. Sprinkle with some of the remaining cheese and pepper and toss gently. Add the croutons and toss just until mixed, so the croutons do not become soggy. Arrange the salad on chilled serving plates and sprinkle lightly with the remaining cheese and pepper.

If you are concerned about using raw eggs, use eggs pasteurized in their shells, which are sold at some specialty food stores, or use an equivalent amount of pasteurized egg substitute. Serves 4.

Courtesy of Damian's Cucina Italiana

Chopped Arugula Summer Salad

Dijon Balsamic Vinaigrette
2 tablespoons chopped shallot
1 1/2 tablespoons white
   balsamic vinegar
2 teaspoons fresh lemon juice
1 teaspoon Dijon mustard
1/3 cup olive oil

Salt and freshly cracked pepper
   to taste

Summer Salad
2 ears sweet corn with husks
1 cup packed coarsely
   chopped arugula
1 cucumber, peeled, seeded
   and chopped

2 large tomatoes, seeded
   and chopped
3 cups packed finely chopped
   mixed salad greens
1/4 to 1/2 cup (1 to 2 ounces)
   shredded Parmesan
   cheese, such as Parmigiano-
   Reggiano cheese

Preheat the oven to 350 degrees.

For the vinaigrette, combine the shallot, vinegar, lemon juice and Dijon mustard in a food processor. Pulse to combine. Add the olive oil gradually and pulse until emulsified. Season with salt and pepper.

For the salad, roast the corn in the husks for about 40 minutes. Let stand until cool. Remove the husks and silk and cut the corn kernels off the cob into a bowl using a sharp knife. Toss the corn, arugula, cucumber, tomatoes, mixed salad greens and cheese in a glass bowl. Add the desired amount of the vinaigrette just before serving and mix well. For a more dramatic presentation, layer the ingredients in a trifle bowl.

For variety, top the salad with leftover cooked chicken or shrimp. Substitute crumbled goat cheese or feta cheese for the Parmesan cheese. Any remaining vinaigrette may be used as a marinade. Serves 4.

Photograph for this recipe on facing page.

Italian Hearts Salad

Parmesan Dressing
6 tablespoons grated
    Parmesan cheese
6 tablespoons white wine vinegar
6 tablespoons lemon juice
2 tablespoons sugar

2 teaspoons salt
1 teaspoon dry mustard
1/2 teaspoon pepper
1 cup olive oil

Hearts Salad
1 (14-ounce) can artichoke
    hearts, drained

1 (7-ounce) jar hearts of
    palm, drained
1 large head romaine, or 3 romaine
    hearts, chopped
1 (4-ounce) jar pimentos, drained

For the dressing, combine the cheese, vinegar, lemon juice, sugar, salt, dry mustard and pepper in a food processor and process until combined. Add the olive oil gradually, processing constantly until emulsified. Whisk the dressing just before adding to the salad as it will separate if not used immediately.

For the salad, chop the artichoke hearts and slice the hearts of palm. Toss the artichokes, hearts of palm, romaine and pimentos in a large salad bowl. Add the desired amount of the dressing and mix until coated. Serves 8.

My parent's garage was like shopping in a second-hand store, you never knew what you would find. I rescued two tables from Houston's heat and humidity, anxious to find uses for them. One of the tables has always been our kitchen table; it has legs similar to a golf club's "wood" (some would say Queen Anne legs, but since my dad was a golfer I would simply say "wood"). With four leaves it is generous enough for our family during those busy nights full of homework, school projects, mail, etc. But it is also plenty big to share with others. Our table is special because it has precious memories etched into it; you can simply look at it and reminisce old times. Every baby and carrier has sat on that table. One Christmas I was given a hedgehog, which ran all over the table. Its prickly body scurrying through our hands—we laughed so hard. We will always cherish the times we've had around that table. The second table, a gate leg table, was a piece I knew I could use anywhere. It has a checkered past, including being used as a TV stand, half open as a desk, and a support for our daughters to lean on while learning to walk. Now it is used as a sofa table, full of those Kodak moments of our friends and family. We hope our daughters will treasure these tables and consider them a blank canvas for their memories to come! —S. Diehl

Asparagus Strawberry Salad

Poppy Seed Dressing

1/4 cup sugar

2 tablespoons cider vinegar

1/2 teaspoon poppy seeds

3/4 teaspoon finely chopped onion

1/4 teaspoon salt

1/8 teaspoon paprika

1/8 teaspoon Worcestershire sauce

1/4 cup olive oil

Asparagus Strawberry Salad

1 pound asparagus

1/4 teaspoon salt

Kosher salt to taste

1 pint fresh strawberries, sliced

1/3 cup crumbled bleu cheese

This recipe requires 1 hour of refrigeration.

For the dressing, combine the sugar, vinegar, poppy seeds, onion, salt, paprika and Worcestershire sauce in a bowl and whisk until the sugar dissolves. Add the olive oil gradually, whisking constantly until emulsified. Chill, covered, for 1 hour.

For the salad, snap off the woody ends of the asparagus spears and discard. Cook the asparagus in a saucepan of boiling salted water for 6 to 8 minutes or until al dente; drain. Immediately plunge the asparagus in a bowl of ice water to stop the cooking process. Drain and pat dry. Arrange the asparagus on a serving platter and sprinkle with kosher salt. Chill, covered, for 1 hour or longer. Sprinkle with the strawberries and cheese and drizzle with the dressing. Serve with a slotted spoon. Serves 8.

Strawberries

Small, sweet Texas strawberries are picked in early and mid-April from Poteet, south of San Antonio, as well as Gillespie County in the Hill Country, and later in the month in East Texas. They are available mainly at pick-your-own operations, roadside stands, and a few grocery stores. These fresh berries are a great buy for health-conscious consumers and anyone who craves the intense flavor of a just-picked product. Strawberries contain folic acid and phytochemicals thought to reduce the incidence of cancer.

Spinach Salad with Apricot Vinaigrette

Apricot Vinaigrette
1/2 cup vegetable oil
2 tablespoons white wine vinegar
2 tablespoons orange juice
1 tablespoon apricot juice
1/2 teaspoon salt

1/2 teaspoon coriander
1/2 teaspoon freshly ground pepper

Spinach Salad
12 ounces baby spinach
1 pint grape tomatoes,
   cut into halves

1 ripe avocado, chopped
1 small red onion, thinly sliced
1/2 cup chopped dried apricots
1/2 cup chopped pecans, toasted
1 cup crumbled feta cheese or
   goat cheese (optional)

For the vinaigrette, combine the oil, vinegar, orange juice, apricot juice, salt, coriander and pepper in a jar with a tight-fitting lid and seal tightly. Shake to combine.

For the salad, toss the spinach, tomatoes, avocado, onion, apricots and pecans in a salad bowl. Add the vinaigrette and mix until coated. Sprinkle with the cheese. Add grilled chicken for an entrée salad. Serves 4 to 6.

My parents' kitchen table could tell the story of my life! Handcrafted by my dad and grandpa, the table served as my parents' first kitchen table when they got married. When I was little, I had a favorite spot at the table—where I could see my baby brother play in his playpen. We've dyed Easter eggs and eaten lots of birthday cakes at that table. As we got older, that table became the meeting ground for many kids in the neighborhood. We could talk, eat, plan, and feel secure around that table. In high school, that table is where I sat up late at night working on physics and calculus problems with my dad, and I cried there with my parents over frustrations and my friend moving away. We celebrated many a successful volleyball win around that table, and it was there that I broke up with my high school sweetheart. It was at that table my family shared a last breakfast before I left to go out of state for college, and where I learned my childhood dog had died. I sat at that table with my parents after graduating college weighing the pros and cons of accepting a job out of state. Later, my boyfriend sat at that table and asked my dad for my hand in marriage; after our wedding, we shared our first meal as a married couple there, too. It was around that table we gathered to celebrate the birth of our first child. That table holds for me a whole lot of emotion, a lot of happiness, a lot of love, friendship, and memories. It also holds sadness and goodbyes. It has literally given me support when I threw my head down in my hands on that table. It has caught my tears. It is not just a piece of wood—it is a guardian of memories and special times for my family and me.   —L. Dupont

Spinach and Blueberry Salad

Blueberry Dressing
1/2 cup raspberry vinegar
1 shallot
1 tablespoon sugar
1/2 pint blueberries
1 cup olive oil

Spinach Salad
10 ounces spinach, stemmed
1 pint blueberries
1/2 cup pecan pieces, toasted
1/2 cup crumbled bleu cheese

For the dressing, process the vinegar, shallot and sugar in a blender until the shallot is finely chopped. Add the blueberries and process until combined. Pour into a bowl and whisk in the olive oil until emulsified.

For the salad, toss the spinach, blueberries, pecans and cheese in a large salad bowl. Add the dressing and mix until coated. Serve immediately. Serves 4 to 6.

Photograph for this recipe on page 34.

Blueberries

Large, sweet, rabbit-eye blueberries are harvested in East Texas from May to mid-July. Frozen Texas blueberries are available year-round. The amazing blueberry has emerged as nature's number one source of antioxidants among fresh fruits and vegetables. In tests at the USDA Human Nutrition Research Center on Aging at Tufts University in Boston, blueberries surpassed thirty-nine other fruits and vegetables in antioxidants that combat cancer, heart disease, and other illnesses.

Warm Grilled Vegetable Salad

Basil Balsamic Dressing
1/3 cup olive oil
1/3 cup balsamic vinegar
2 garlic cloves
1 teaspoon sugar

1/4 teaspoon salt, or to taste
1/4 cup fresh basil leaves

Vegetable Salad
6 cups fresh baby spinach leaves
1 red onion
3 green or yellow summer squash
1 red or yellow bell pepper

2 cups button mushrooms,
   stemmed
2 teaspoons seasoned salt
1/2 cup chopped oil-pack sun-dried
   tomatoes, drained
1 cup (4 ounces) coarsely grated
   asiago cheese

Preheat the grill on medium.

For the dressing, combine the olive oil, vinegar, garlic, sugar and salt in a blender. Process for 8 to 10 seconds or until puréed; check to make sure no large pieces of garlic remain. Add the basil and pulse three or four times.

For the salad, place the spinach in a large salad bowl. Cut the onion, squash and bell pepper into long wide slices that will fit on the grill without falling through the grill rack. Sprinkle the onion, squash, bell pepper and mushrooms with the seasoned salt and lightly spray with nonstick cooking spray.

Grill the vegetables for a few minutes on each side until tender or to the desired degree of crispness. Cool slightly and then coarsely chop the vegetables. Gently toss the warm vegetables with the spinach. Drizzle with the dressing and sprinkle with the sun-dried tomatoes and cheese. Serve with grilled flat-iron steak, grilled corn on the cob, crusty French bread and a glass of pinot noir. End your meal with grilled peach slices sprinkled with brown sugar and topped with a scoop of vanilla ice cream and a splash of brandy. Serves 8.

Greek Quesadillas

16 ounces cream cheese, softened
2/3 cup mixed kalamata olives and green olives, chopped
12 garlic cloves, roasted and chopped
2 cucumbers, peeled, seeded and thinly sliced
1 purple onion, thinly sliced

3 1/2 tablespoons red wine vinegar
1 teaspoon white pepper
1 teaspoon salt
1 teaspoon dried oregano
6 tablespoons extra-virgin olive oil
4 pita bread rounds
1/2 cup (2 ounces) shredded Cheddar cheese

1/2 cup (2 ounces) shredded Monterey Jack cheese
4 ounces feta cheese, crumbled
1 tablespoon butter
1 teaspoon sesame seeds, toasted (optional)

*T*his recipe requires 30 minutes marinating time. Combine the cream cheese, olives and garlic in a bowl and mix until of a spreading consistency. Mix the cucumbers, onion, wine vinegar, white pepper, salt and oregano in a bowl. Taste and adjust seasonings. Add the olive oil to the cucumber mixture and stir until coated. Marinate at room temperature for 30 minutes or longer.

Open the pita bread rounds by cutting halfway around the edges. Spread the cream cheese mixture about 1/4 inch thick on the inside of one side of each pita round. Layer with the marinated cucumber mixture, Cheddar cheese, Monterey Jack cheese and feta cheese. Pinch the edges to seal.

Lightly butter both sides of the pita rounds. Cook in a skillet over medium-high heat until the cheese melts and the pita rounds are brown on both sides, turning once. Remove to a platter and cut each round into quarters or eighths. Garnish with the sesame seeds. Serve hot. Makes 4 quesadillas.

*W*e love family game nights. One or two nights a month, we alternate letting our three children pick a game. Monopoly and Clue are our favorites. We make appetizers for dinner and play games. After the games we enjoy an awesome homemade dessert. No one misses a night without television, and we are creating tons of great memories! To make it even more festive, our centerpiece is a candle in a hurricane glass. We decorate around the candle with edible treats to coincide with the month (i.e., February would be candy hearts, March would be rainbow Skittles, etc.). Always a treat! —H. Jackson

California Panini

1 round focaccia or basil focaccia
Roasted raspberry chipotle sauce
4 (1/8-inch) slices goat cheese
1 Granny Smith apple, thinly sliced

4 ounces smoked turkey,
   thinly sliced
1 tablespoon olive oil

*P*reheat a panini grill. Slice the focaccia round into halves. Brush the cut sides with chipotle marinade. Layer the cheese slices, apple and turkey evenly on the bottom round and top with remaining round. Coat the focaccia with the olive oil.

Cook using the manufacturers' directions or until golden brown. If you do not have a panini grill, place the sandwich in a skillet and top the sandwich with a brick wrapped in foil. Cook over medium-high heat until the cheese melts and the sandwich is golden brown on both sides. Cut into halves. Serves 2.

Caprese Panini

2 to 4 tablespoons Basil Pesto
   (page 53) or commercially-
   prepared pesto
2 slices sourdough bread

2 (1/4-inch) slices beefsteak tomato
2 (1/4-inch) slices fresh
   mozzarella cheese
2 basil leaves

*S*pread the pesto on one side of each slice of bread. Layer the tomato, cheese and basil leaves on the pesto side of one slice of the bread and top with the remaining bread slice pesto side down. Grill in a grill pan or panini maker. Cut the sandwich into halves and serve. For a festive look, wrap each half in baking parchment.

You may prepare the sandwiches in advance, wrap in baking parchment and store in the refrigerator. Warm in the oven just before serving. Or for a salad, omit the bread, tear the basil and mix all the ingredients in a salad bowl. Serves 1.

Photograph for these recipes on facing page.

Apples

The longer apples stay on the tree, the higher their sugar content and thus the sweeter their flavor. That is why no apples even come close to tree-ripened Texas apples, which are up to 40 percent sweeter than other apples. Because the apples ripen during the hot Texas summer, they do not develop the fruit's typical deep red color. Quality, however, is extremely high. Harvest starts in late June, when other apples come from cold storage, and ends in November.

Pork and Black Bean Wrap

Pork Tenderloin

3 garlic cloves, coarsely chopped
1 canned chipotle pepper in
    adobo sauce, seeded and
    coarsely chopped
2 tablespoons fresh lime juice
1/2 teaspoon dried oregano
1 (14-ounce) pork tenderloin
Salt and pepper to taste

Black Bean Salsa

1 (15-ounce) can black beans,
    drained and rinsed
1 yellow bell pepper, chopped
2 scallions, thinly sliced
1/4 cup chopped fresh cilantro
3 tablespoons fresh lime juice
1 teaspoon extra-virgin olive oil
1 teaspoon ground cumin
Salt and pepper to taste

Cilantro Aïoli and Assembly

1 cup mayonnaise
Juice of 1 lime
1 1/2 tablespoons chopped
    fresh cilantro
4 whole wheat tortillas
1 ripe avocado, thinly sliced

Chipotle peppers are dried, smoked jalapeño peppers canned in a piquant adobo sauce. They lend a spicy, smoky flavor to this pork and black bean wrap. Remember to remove the seeds from the peppers before chopping, and rinse your hands well after handling the peppers.

This recipe requires 1 hour of refrigeration. Preheat the oven to 350 degrees.

For the tenderloin, process the garlic, chipotle pepper, lime juice and oregano in a blender until puréed. Season the pork with salt and pepper and place in a sealable plastic bag. Add the chipotle pepper purée to the bag and seal tightly. Turn to coat. Marinate in the refrigerator for 1 hour or longer, turning occasionally.

Coat a large ovenproof nonstick skillet with nonstick cooking spray and heat over high heat. Sear the pork on all sides in the hot skillet for about 6 minutes. Bake for 20 minutes or until a meat thermometer registers 160 degrees. Let the pork rest for 5 minutes and then thinly slice. Maintain the oven temperature.

For the salsa, combine the beans, bell pepper, scallions, cilantro, lime juice, olive oil, cumin, salt and pepper in a large bowl and mix gently.

For the aïoli, combine the mayonnaise, lime juice and cilantro in a bowl and mix well. Store, covered, in the refrigerator until serving time. Wrap the tortillas in foil and warm in the oven.

Invite your guests to prepare their own wraps with the tortillas, sliced pork, salsa, aïoli and avocado. Or, you can layer the ingredients on the tortillas and sprinkle with shredded Pepper Jack cheese. Fold in half and heat in a skillet like a quesadilla. Serves 4.

Ciabatta Ham Sandwich with Pesto and Roasted Poblano

1/2 onion, sliced
2 tablespoons olive oil
1/2 teaspoon sugar
1/8 to 1/4 cup Basil Pesto (page 53)

1 ciabatta roll, cut into halves
3 or 4 slices honey-roasted ham or
smoked ham

3 (1/4-inch) round slices fresh
mozzarella cheese
1/2 poblano pepper, roasted, peeled
and seeded

Sauté the onion in the olive oil in a skillet for 15 minutes. Add the sugar and
continue to sauté until the onion is caramelized.

Spread the pesto on the cut sides of the roll. Layer the bottom half with the ham,
cheese, poblano pepper and 2 tablespoons of the caramelized onion. Top with the remaining
roll half. Bake in a sandwich maker using the manufacturer's directions or grill in a grill
pan or sauté pan. Top with the remaining caramelized onion. Makes 1 sandwich.

Photograph for this recipe on page 68.

> ### Ciabatta Bread—
> ### What Does It Mean?
>
> *Ciabatta means "slipper"
> due to its shape (literally
> "carpet slipper"). A
> "panino" is a sandwich
> (plural: panini) commonly
> made with ciabatta
> bread, but other breads
> can be substituted as well.*

Miniature Reuben Bites

24 slices party rye bread
1/2 cup Worcestershire sauce
3 tablespoons minced onion

1/2 cup Thousand Island
salad dressing
8 ounces pastrami, thinly sliced

8 ounces Swiss cheese, thinly sliced
1/2 cup alfalfa sprouts (optional)

Preheat the oven to 400 degrees. Arrange the bread slices in a single layer on a
lightly greased or nonstick baking sheet. Mix the Worcestershire sauce and onion in a bowl.
Baste one side of each of the bread slices with the Worcestershire sauce mixture. Top each
slice with 1 teaspoon of the salad dressing.

Cut the pastrami slices and cheese slices into 2-inch pieces to cover the bread slices.
Layer each slice with one piece of the pastrami and one piece of the cheese. Bake for
5 minutes or until the cheese melts. Top with the sprouts. Makes 2 dozen bites.

Curry Chicken Sandwich

14 cups water
20 whole black peppercorns
2 bay leaves
2 whole cloves
1/2 lemon
3 pounds chicken tenders

1/2 cup plus 2 tablespoons spicy
  brown mustard
1/2 cup honey
1 1/4 teaspoons curry powder
3/4 teaspoon lemon pepper
1/8 teaspoon salt
1 loaf challah or rich egg bread,
  cut into 12 thick slices

Butter, softened
1/2 cup shredded carrots
1/2 cup slivered almonds
2 tomatoes, chopped
Mesclun
Red grapes or assorted berries
  (optional)

This recipe requires 30 minutes of refrigeration. Combine the water, peppercorns, bay leaves, cloves and lemon in a stockpot. Cover and bring to a boil over high heat. Add the chicken and cook for 7 to 10 minutes or until the chicken is cooked through, stirring occasionally. Drain, discarding the solids and reserving the chicken. Cool the chicken and cut each chicken tender crosswise into quarters.

Combine the mustard, honey, curry powder, lemon pepper and salt in a bowl and mix well. Stir in the chicken. Chill, covered, for 30 minutes or for up to 1 day.

Spread both sides of the bread slices with butter. Heat a nonstick skillet over medium-high heat. Cook the bread in batches in the hot skillet for 3 to 5 minutes or until brown on both sides, turning once.

Stir the carrots and almonds into the chicken mixture. Mound the chicken mixture evenly on six slices of the bread on serving plates. Layer evenly with the tomatoes, mesclun and remaining bread slices. Garnish with grapes and/or assorted berries. Makes 6 sandwiches.

Photograph for this recipe on page 68.

Party Pistolettes

16 unsliced whole wheat
   hoagie rolls
1 (10-ounce) package frozen
   chopped broccoli
1 1/2 pounds ground beef

1 onion, chopped
1 1/2 tablespoons Creole seasoning
1 pound Velveeta cheese, cubed
3/4 cup (1 1/2 sticks) butter
1 teaspoon garlic powder

Preheat the oven to 400 degrees. Cut the rolls into halves and remove the centers. Cook the broccoli using the package directions; drain.

Brown the ground beef with the onion in a skillet, stirring until the ground beef is crumbly; drain. Mix in the Creole seasoning. Add the cheese and cook until the cheese melts, stirring frequently. Stir in the broccoli.

Stuff the roll halves with the ground beef mixture and reassemble the tops and bottoms. Arrange the stuffed rolls 2 inches apart on a baking sheet. Melt the butter in a saucepan and stir in the garlic powder. Brush the rolls with the butter mixture. Bake for 10 to 15 minutes or until golden brown.

You may prepare early in the day and store, covered, in the refrigerator. Brush with the butter mixture just before baking. Or, freeze for future use and bake just before serving. Makes 16 pistolettes.

The Buffet Table

Dating back to the third century B.C., Athenians served small pieces of seafood coated in spices prior to the main meal. Today, tempting the eye and teasing the taste buds, appetizers, or "hors d'oeuvre", are often served buffet-style, offering a variety of flavor, color, and texture and utilizing all food groups to stimulate our appetites. Modern appetizers give the ancient culinary invention a remarkable new twenty-first century trend for whetting the appetite or serving as tidbits to nibble while socializing with friends and family.

> *"The appetite is sharpened by the first bites."*
>
> —Jose Rizal

Ceviche	78	91	Sweet Jammin' Salsa
Asian Tuna Tartare	79	91	Best Salsa
Grilled Bacon-Wrapped Chipotle Shrimp	79	92	Seafood Cheesecake
Asian Chicken on Endive	81	93	Marinated Goat Cheese Log
Gulf Coast Chardonnay Oysters	83	93	Pesto Panna Formaggio
Spicy Rosemary Almonds	83	95	Mango Chutney Torta
Friday Night Focaccia	84	96	Cremini Bouchées
Southern Caviar	85	97	Chicken Satay with Spicy Peanut Sauce
Artichoke Pesto	85	98	Duck Turnovers
Creamy Corn Dip	87	99	Savory Prosciutto and Fig Tartlets
Three Onion Dip with Gaufrette Potato Chips	87	99	Crab Rangoon
"Love It" Dip	88	100	Fried Green Tomatoes with Crab Meat Rémoulade
Penman's Party Dip	88	101	Vietnamese Spring Rolls
Avocado Feta Salsa	89	101	Spicy Pretzels
Red Room Spinach and Feta Dip	89		

Ceviche

1 pound mild white fish,
    such as tilapia
1/4 cup fresh lemon juice
1/4 cup fresh lime juice

1 small red onion, finely
    chopped (about 1 1/2 cups)
2 cups chopped seeded peeled
    beefsteak tomatoes
1/4 cup chopped cilantro
1 1/2 tablespoons apple
    cider vinegar

3 tablespoons olive oil
3 to 6 teaspoons minced
    jalapeño pepper
1 teaspoon chopped fresh oregano
1/2 teaspoon ground cumin
1/4 teaspoon salt
1/4 teaspoon pepper

*T*his recipe requires 3 hours of refrigeration. Cut the fish into bite-size pieces. Place the fish in a shallow nonreactive dish. Add the lemon juice and lime juice and toss gently until coated. Marinate, covered, in the refrigerator for 2 hours.

Add the onion, tomatoes, cilantro, vinegar, olive oil, jalapeño chile, oregano, cumin, salt and pepper to the fish mixture and mix gently. Marinate, covered, for 1 to 2 hours longer. Serve chilled alone or with tortilla chips. Serves 10.

Photograph for this recipe on page 74.

As an adult looking back on my childhood, I remember some of the most random moments . . . our family dog, Champagne (named for the cockapoo's color), my sister's black, curly, ringlet-filled head (which I loved to brush) . . . and the honey-colored French country dining room table that resided in our dining room for as long as I can remember. It sat patiently, ready to welcome our family and the spread of food that came with us at each sitting. My mom always dressed the table for each occasion with cloths and placemats and on very special occasions, napkins and napkin rings. It was our very own, scaled-down version of tablescaping, before it was termed! I remember the times around the table more than the food served . . . although my mom's lasagna and several turkeys do come to mind.

Transferred to Texas as a young girl, our family of five comfortably indulged in dinner, dessert, and most memorable reminiscence during those precious moments around our family's table. That table now sits in my sister's home. Freshly painted and distressed black, it sits looking so very modern and trendy nearly twenty-five years later. I look forward to holidays at her home, where the now twelve of us (we've added three spouses and four children) will once again take places around our family's rectangular table and reminisce and create new memories. —M. Herndon

Asian Tuna Tartare

4 ounces saku tuna, cut into
  1/4-inch pieces
2 tablespoons finely chopped
  green onions
1 tablespoon finely chopped
  fresh ginger

1 tablespoon finely chopped
  yellow onion
2 tablespoons teriyaki sauce
1 tablespoon sweet chili sauce
1 teaspoon sesame oil
1 teaspoon black and white sesame
  seeds, toasted

1/4 teaspoon sea salt
1/8 teaspoon pepper
8 fried won ton chips
  (rectangular cut)
1 chive tip (optional)
Paprika to taste

Combine the tuna, green onions, ginger and yellow onion in a small stainless steel bowl and mix gently. Stir in the teriyaki sauce, chili sauce, sesame oil, sesame seeds, salt and pepper.

Pack the tartare into a cheesecake mold until filled. Arrange on a serving plate and remove the mold carefully; do not break the tuna tower. Encircle the tower with the won ton chips facing the same direction. Garnish the top with the chive tip. Sprinkle paprika around the edge of the plate. Serves 1.

Courtesy of Perry's Steakhouse and Grille

> *A two-inch piece of PVC pipe works great as a mold and also is good for stacked salads.*

Grilled Bacon-Wrapped Chipotle Shrimp

Sliced bacon (1 slice per shrimp)
1 pound shrimp, peeled
  and deveined

Pepper Jack cheese, cut into
  1/8 × 1-inch strips
3 jalapeño peppers, cut into
  1/8 × 1-inch strips

1 1/2 bottles Roasted Raspberry
  Chipotle sauce

Preheat the oven to 350 degrees. Preheat the grill. Arrange bacon in a single layer on a baking sheet with sides. Bake for 7 minutes or until partially cooked. Let stand until cool.

Butterfly the shrimp to form a small pocket in each. Insert one cheese strip and one jalapeño pepper strip in each shrimp. Wrap tightly with one slice of the bacon and thread on a skewer. Brush both sides of the shrimp with the sauce. Let stand for 10 minutes. Grill over indirect heat until the shrimp turn pink. Serve as an appetizer or as a main entrée over hot cooked rice. Variable servings.

Asian Chicken on Endive

1 cup soy sauce
1 cup packed light brown sugar
4 teaspoons white vinegar
2 tablespoons dark sesame oil
1 1/2 pounds chicken tenders
1 (8-ounce) can water chestnuts, drained

2 cups shiitake mushrooms, stemmed and sliced
1 tablespoon dark sesame oil
1/4 cup thinly sliced scallions
2 teaspoons minced garlic
24 Belgian endive spears

Mix the soy sauce, brown sugar and vinegar in a bowl until the brown sugar dissolves. Heat 2 tablespoons sesame oil in a wok or large skillet over high heat. Sauté the chicken in the hot oil for 4 to 5 minutes per side or until cooked through. Remove the chicken to a platter to cool, reserving the pan drippings. Mince the water chestnuts, mushrooms and cooled chicken to the size of small peas.

Heat the reserved pan drippings with 1 tablespoon sesame oil until hot. Add the mushrooms and cook for 5 minutes or until all the moisture has evaporated. Stir in the chicken, water chestnuts, scallions and garlic.

Cook until heated through, stirring frequently. Serve in endive spears as an appetizer, or in lettuce cups for a hearty meal. Drizzle with the soy sauce mixture. Serve with chile sauce such as sambal. Or, make your own sauce by combing soy sauce, white vinegar, Chinese hot mustard, chile paste and chile oil in the proportions desired. Makes 2 dozen.

Photograph for this recipe on facing page.

This dish can be made in advance. Prepare the chicken and chill in an airtight container for up to two days. Prepare the endive spears, wrap in damp paper towels, and store in a sealable plastic bag for eight to ten hours. Just before serving, reheat the chicken and fill the endive spears.

Gulf Coast Chardonnay Oysters

24 fresh oysters on the half shell
2 shallots, minced
1 tablespoon unsalted butter
1 cup chardonnay

1 cup heavy cream
1 teaspoon Madras curry
Salt and pepper to taste

Preheat the oven to 450 degrees. Drain the oysters, reserving the liquor. Sauté the shallots in the butter in a medium saucepan for 1 minute. Add the wine and bring to a boil. Reduce the heat and simmer for 6 to 8 minutes or until the liquid is reduced by half. Stir in the reserved oyster liquor.

Cook for 2 minutes. Strain into a saucepan, discarding the solids. Stir in the cream and bring to a slow boil. Reduce the heat and simmer for 10 to 12 minutes or until the liquid is reduced by half. Stir in the curry and salt.

Arrange the oysters in the shells in a single layer in a roasting pan. Sprinkle with pepper. Top each oyster with 1 tablespoon of the wine sauce. Bake for 4 to 5 minutes or until the sauce begins to brown and the edges of the oysters curl. Serves 8.

Photograph for this recipe on facing page.

Spicy Rosemary Almonds

1¼ pounds whole almonds with
   skins, or 1¼ pounds cashews
   or peanuts
3 tablespoons coarsely chopped
   fresh rosemary leaves

2 tablespoons kosher salt
2 teaspoons dark brown sugar
1½ teaspoons cayenne pepper
1 tablespoon butter, melted

Preheat the oven to 375 degrees. Spread the almonds in a single layer on a baking sheet. Bake for about 10 minutes or until the almonds are heated through.

Mix the rosemary, salt, brown sugar and cayenne pepper in a bowl. Stir in the butter. Add the warm almonds and toss until completely coated. Serve warm. Serves 8 to 10.

Shucking Oysters

To shuck oysters, hold a strong oyster knife in your dominant hand. With the opposite hand covered in a glove or mitt, hold the oyster rounded side down with the pointed end facing you. Push the knife blade in the indentation between the upper and lower shells. Slide the knife away from the hinge and twist until the shell cracks. Lift the top shell and sever the connector muscle before running the knife underneath the oyster to sever that connector. The liquor around the oyster must be clear, not milky, and the scent pleasant and appealing.

Friday Night Focaccia

5 garlic cloves
1 tablespoon olive oil
1 cup warm water
1 envelope fast-rising yeast
2 tablespoons sugar

3 1/2 cup to 4 cups
    all-purpose flour
1 tablespoon coarse salt
2 tablespoons water
1/4 cup olive oil
2 tablespoons finely chopped
    fresh rosemary
2 tablespoons olive oil
Olive oil for coating and brushing

1/4 cup cornmeal
1 onion, thinly sliced
1 tablespoon olive oil
1 to 1 1/2 roasted red bell peppers,
    peeled, seeded and cut into
    thin strips
1/4 cup (1 ounce) grated
    Parmesan cheese
Freshly ground pepper to taste

This recipe requires 45 minutes of rising time. Preheat the oven to 350 degrees. Place the garlic on a sheet of foil large enough to enclose. Drizzle the garlic with 1 tablespoon olive oil and seal tightly. Place the foil packet on a baking sheet and roast for 20 minutes. Let stand until cool and then mash the garlic. Increase the oven temperature to 400 degrees.

Combine 1 cup warm water, the yeast and sugar in a mixing bowl of a standing mixer fitted with a dough hook. Stir gently to dissolve the yeast and sugar. Let stand for 3 minutes or until foamy. Add the flour gradually, mixing constantly at low speed and scraping the side of the bowl as needed. Dissolve the salt in 2 tablespoons water in a bowl and add to the flour mixture. Mix until blended. Add 1/4 cup olive oil just as the dough begins to adhere and slowly increase the mixer speed to medium. Beat for about 10 minutes, scraping the side of the bowl as needed and adding the rosemary 1 minute before the end of the process.

Turn the dough onto a lightly floured hard surface and fold over several times. Shape the dough into a ball and coat with 2 tablespoons olive oil. Place the dough in a large bowl. Fill the kitchen sink with 4 inches of warm to hot water and place the bowl in the water. Cover the dough with a tea towel. Let rise for 45 minutes or until doubled in bulk.

Coat a baking sheet with olive oil and sprinkle with the cornmeal. Turn the dough onto a lightly floured surface and roll into a 1/2-inch-thick rectangle. Place the rectangle on the prepared baking sheet. Let rest for 15 minutes.

Sauté the onion in 1 tablespoon olive oil in a skillet over low heat for about 15 minutes or until the onion is caramelized. Dimple the dough with your fingertips and brush with olive oil. Spread the mashed garlic over the top. Sprinkle with the bell peppers, caramelized onion, cheese and pepper. Bake for 15 to 20 minutes or until light brown. Cut into 1 1/2-inch squares and serve warm. Great served with olive oil infused with chopped basil and ground pepper. Serves 10.

Southern Caviar

2 (16-ounce) cans black-eyed
    peas, drained
2 (11-ounce) cans Shoe Peg
    corn, drained
1 green bell pepper, chopped

1 yellow bell pepper, chopped
1 red bell pepper, chopped
2 (10-ounce) cans diced tomatoes
    with green chiles, drained
1 teaspoon garlic powder

1 or 2 bunches green
    onions, chopped
1 large bottle Italian salad dressing
1 large avocado, chopped
    (optional)

This recipe requires 8 hours of refrigeration. Mix the peas, corn, bell peppers, tomatoes, garlic powder and green onions in a bowl. Add the salad dressing and mix until combined.

Chill, covered, for 8 to 10 hours, stirring occasionally. Drain the "caviar" and stir in the avocado just before serving. Serve with tortilla chips. Serves 24.

Artichoke Pesto

2 (14-ounce) cans artichoke
    hearts, drained
1 tablespoon olive oil
Kosher salt and cracked pepper
    to taste

2 tablespoons pine nuts, toasted
8 garlic cloves
40 large fresh basil leaves
4 to 5 tablespoons olive oil

2 tablespoons grated
    Parmesan cheese
1 teaspoon fresh lemon juice

Preheat the oven to 350 degrees. Coat the artichokes with 1 tablespoon olive oil and sprinkle with salt and pepper. Arrange the artichokes in a single layer on a baking sheet. Roast for 20 to 25 minutes. Let stand until cool.

Combine the pine nuts, garlic and a sprinkle of salt in a food processor. Add the basil, processing constantly. Turn off the food processor and stir. Add the artichokes, 4 to 5 tablespoons olive oil, the cheese and lemon juice and process to the desired consistency. Season with salt and pepper. Serve with bagel chips or baguette slices. Store, covered, for up to 2 days in the refrigerator.

If the flavor of garlic is too strong, substitute roasted garlic for the garlic cloves. Add additional olive oil for a thinner consistency or more Parmesan cheese for a thicker consistency. Makes 2 cups.

Great served over hot cooked pasta or used as a spread on ham sandwiches.

Creamy Corn Dip

4 ears fresh corn
1 red bell pepper, finely chopped
1 shallot or small onion,
　finely chopped
3 garlic cloves, chopped

2 tablespoons butter
8 ounces cream cheese, softened
4 to 6 slices pancetta or bacon,
　crisp-cooked and crumbled
1/4 cup mayonnaise

2 or 3 jalapeño peppers seeded
　and chopped
Salt and pepper to taste
4 ounces sharp Cheddar
　cheese, shredded

*P*reheat the oven to 400 degrees. Cut the corn kernels off the cob into a bowl using
a sharp knife. Sauté the corn, bell pepper, shallot and garlic in the butter in an ovenproof
saucepan over medium heat until the shallot and bell pepper are tender. Reduce the heat
to low. Stir in the cream cheese, pancetta, mayonnaise, jalapeño peppers, salt and pepper.
Simmer until well combined. Sprinkle with the cheese. Bake until the cheese melts and the
dip is heated through. Serve warm with corn chips. For a tailgate appetizer, heat in a cast-
iron skillet on a grill. Serves 12.

Three Onion Dip with Gaufrette Potato Chips

3 cups julienned yellow onions
3 cups julienned red onions
1/4 cup olive oil
1 tablespoon sugar
1 tablespoon sherry vinegar

2 cups sour cream
1/4 cup milk
2 tablespoons chopped green onions
1 tablespoon kosher salt
1 teaspoon freshly cracked pepper

Chopped green onion tops
　(optional)
3 or 4 Idaho potatoes, peeled
Vegetable oil
Kosher salt to taste

*S*auté the julienned onions in the olive oil in a skillet over medium heat for 20 to
30 minutes or until the onions are caramelized and dark brown, adding the sugar just as
they begin to caramelize. Stir in the vinegar. Cook until the vinegar evaporates. Let
stand until cool. Reserve some of the onions for garnish. Combine the caramelized onions
with the sour cream, milk, 2 tablespoons green onions, 1 tablespoon salt and the pepper in
a bowl; mix well. Top with the reserved onions and green onion tops. Cut the potatoes
into 1/8- to 1/4-inch slices using a mandoline. Rotate the potatoes 45 degrees and slice
again to create a waffle pattern. Heat vegetable oil in a deep skillet to 350 degrees. Add
the potatoes and fry until light brown and crisp. Drain on paper towels and sprinkle with
salt. Serve with the onion dip. Serves 16.

Photograph for this recipe on facing page.

"Love It" Dip

16 ounces cream cheese, softened
1/2 cup salsa
1 tablespoon chopped
   fresh cilantro

1 teaspoon onion powder
1/2 teaspoon cayenne pepper
1 teaspoon dehydrated
   minced garlic

1/2 teaspoon crumbled
   dried tarragon
1/2 teaspoon kosher salt
1/4 teaspoon white pepper

This recipe requires several hours of refrigeration. Combine the cream cheese, salsa, cilantro, onion powder, cayenne pepper, garlic, tarragon, salt and white pepper in a mixing bowl. Beat until combined and of a dip consistency.

Chill, covered, for several hours to allow the flavors to meld. Serve with bread and/or assorted sturdy crackers. Serves 8.

Penman's Party Dip

16 ounces cream cheese, softened
1/2 cup (1 stick) butter, softened
8 ounces Gruyère cheese, grated
10 slices bacon or pancetta, crisp-
   cooked and crumbled
3 jalapeño peppers, finely chopped

4 Roma tomatoes, seeded
   and chopped
1/2 teaspoon salt
1/2 teaspoon freshly cracked pepper
3/4 cup (3 ounces) grated
   Parmesan cheese

Preheat the oven to 350 degrees. Combine the cream cheese and butter in a bowl and mix until uniform in color. Fold in the Gruyère cheese, bacon, jalapeño peppers, tomatoes, salt and pepper. (Seeded tomatoes are necessary to prevent a watery dip.)

Spread the cheese mixture in a deep round baking dish. Sprinkle with the Parmesan cheese. Bake for 30 to 45 minutes or until the Parmesan cheese is brown. Serve warm with corn scoops or baguette slices. Serves 20.

Avocado Feta Salsa

1 cup chopped seeded
   plum tomatoes
4 ounces feta cheese, crumbled
   into large pieces
3 tablespoons red wine vinegar

2 tablespoons olive oil
2 tablespoons finely chopped
   red onion
2 garlic cloves, minced
1 tablespoon chopped parsley

1/2 teaspoon dried oregano
1/2 teaspoon salt
2 avocados, chopped

Combine the tomatoes, cheese, vinegar, olive oil, onion, garlic, parsley, oregano and salt in a bowl. Mix gently to prevent breaking up the cheese. Fold in the avocados. Serve immediately with tortilla chips, or store, covered, in the refrigerator. If preparing in advance and storing in the refrigerator, fold the avocados into the salsa just before serving to prevent discoloration. Serves 6.

Red Room Spinach and Feta Dip

20 ounces cream cheese, softened
4 ounces fresh spinach, stemmed
   and chopped
1 cup crumbled feta cheese

1/2 cup chopped red onion
2 tablespoons minced garlic
Salt to taste

Preheat the oven to 350 degrees. Combine the cream cheese, spinach, feta cheese, onion and garlic in a mixing bowl and beat until combined. Season with salt.

Spread the cream cheese mixture in a baking dish. Bake for 20 minutes or until light brown and bubbly. Serve hot with toasted pita wedges. Serves 12.

Garlic

Choose garlic heads that are plump and firm with no discolorations. To peel garlic cloves, lightly crush with the flat side of a chef's knife and remove the skin. Before slicing or mincing, remove the root end and any green sprouting as that may impart a bitter flavor. And never cook garlic beyond a light golden color as that produces a harsh flavor.

Sweet Jammin' Salsa

4 habanero peppers
2 cups mango preserves or peach
    preserves or spread
2 cups crushed pineapple
Juice of 2 Key limes

4 teaspoons sugar
1 teaspoon kosher salt
1 teaspoon cider vinegar
1 red bell pepper, chopped
4 green onions, finely chopped

This recipe requires refrigeration time. Preheat the broiler to 425 degrees. Arrange the habanero peppers on a baking sheet. Broil for 8 minutes or until charred on all sides, turning frequently. Let stand until cool. Finely chop the habanero peppers, discarding the skin, membranes and seeds.

Combine the preserves, pineapple, lime juice, sugar, salt and vinegar in a bowl and mix well. Stir in the habanero peppers, bell pepper and green onions. Serve chilled with tortilla chips. Always wear gloves when handling habanero chiles, as they can seriously burn the skin. For a thinner consistency, heat the preserves in a saucepan prior to mixing. Serves 20.

Photograph for this recipe on facing page.

Best Salsa

3 pounds Roma tomatoes
1 yellow onion, cut into halves
2 jalapeño peppers
2 garlic cloves, finely chopped
2 tablespoons olive oil

1 teaspoon salt
2 to 4 tablespoons chopped
    fresh cilantro
1 tablespoon fresh lime juice
Freshly cracked pepper to taste

Preheat the grill. Roast the tomatoes, onion and jalapeño peppers on a gas grill or gas cooktop until charred on all sides and soft. Cool slightly. Remove the seeds and stems of the jalapeño peppers.

Combine the tomatoes, onion, jalapeño peppers, garlic, olive oil and salt in a food processor or blender. Pulse to the desired consistency. Add the cilantro, lime juice and pepper and pulse to combine. Serve with tortilla chips. Serves 12.

Seafood Cheesecake

1/2 cup (1 stick) butter, melted
1 1/2 cups saltine cracker crumbs
Salt and pepper to taste
32 ounces cream cheese, softened
2 egg yolks
2 eggs

1 tablespoon cornstarch
6 tablespoons heavy
    whipping cream
2 1/2 tablespoons Basil Pesto
    (page 53) or commercially
    prepared pesto
1 teaspoon salt
1/2 teaspoon pepper

4 ounces cooked shrimp,
    finely chopped
4 to 8 ounces lump crab meat,
    drained and shells removed
1 tablespoon Basil Pesto (page 53)
    or commercially prepared
    pesto (optional)

*T*his recipe requires 8 hours of refrigeration. Preheat the oven to 350 degrees. Coat the side and bottom of a 6-inch springform pan with nonstick cooking pray. Wrap foil around the bottom of the pan.

Mix the butter and crackers in a bowl until well combined. Season with salt and pepper to taste. Pat the crumb mixture over the bottom of the prepared pan. Bake for 8 minutes or until light brown.

Beat the cream cheese in a mixing bowl until creamy. Add the egg yolks and eggs one at a time, beating well after each addition. Place the cornstarch in a small cup and gradually mix in the cream until blended. Add to the cream cheese mixture and beat until blended. Mix in 2 1/2 tablespoons Pesto, 1 teaspoon salt and 1/2 teaspoon pepper.

Reserve a small amount of the shrimp and crab meat for garnish. Stir the remaining shrimp and the remaining crab meat into the cream cheese mixture. Spread the shrimp mixture over the baked layer. Place the springform pan in a larger baking pan and add enough water to the baking pan to come halfway up the side of the springform pan.

Bake for 1 hour. Turn off the oven. Let the cheesecake stand in the oven with the door closed for 20 minutes. Remove from the oven and let stand until cool. Chill for 8 to 10 hours. To serve, remove the side of the springform pan and top with the reserved shrimp and the reserved crab meat. Garnish with 1 tablespoon Pesto. Serve with assorted party crackers and/or pita chips. Serves 8 to 12.

Marinated Goat Cheese Log

1 (16-ounce) log goat cheese
2 tablespoons cracked
    black pepper
1 tablespoon red pepper flakes
1 cup (or more) olive oil

1 cup chopped sun-dried tomatoes
1/2 cup finely chopped roasted red
    bell pepper
1/2 cup red onion strips

2 tablespoons chiffonade fresh basil
2 tablespoons chopped
    fresh parsley
4 garlic cloves, minced

*T*his recipe requires 8 hours of refrigeration. Place the cheese log in a container with sides and a lid just large enough to hold the log. Sprinkle the entire surface of the log with the black pepper and red pepper flakes. Combine the olive oil, sun-dried tomatoes, bell pepper, onion, basil, parsley and garlic in a bowl and mix well. Pour the olive oil mixture over the goat cheese, adding additional olive oil if needed to cover the cheese log. Marinate, sealed tightly, for 8 hours or longer. Serve at room temperature with assorted party crackers. Toss any leftovers with warm cooked pasta. Discard the red onion, if desired. Serves 8 to 10.

Photograph for this recipe on page 74.

Pesto Panna Formaggio

10 thin slices provolone cheese
16 ounces cream cheese, softened
6 garlic cloves, finely chopped

10 ounces oil-pack sun-dried
    tomatoes, drained and chopped

10 ounces Basil Pesto (page 53) or
    commercially prepared pesto

*T*his recipe requires 8 hours of refrigeration. Line a 5×7-inch loaf pan with plastic wrap, allowing enough overhang to fold over the top. Line the prepared loaf pan with seven slices of the provolone cheese, overlapping up the sides to cover. The provolone cheese will act as the outer shell of the torta.

Beat the cream cheese and garlic in a mixing bowl until light and fluffy. Spread half the cream cheese mixture in the prepared pan. Layer with two-thirds of the sun-dried tomatoes, two-thirds of the Pesto and the remaining cream cheese mixture. Top with the remaining three slices of provolone cheese, completely covering the top. There may be some overlapping of the side cheese slices with the top cheese slices. Pull the plastic wrap over the top to cover. Chill for 8 to 10 hours or until firm. Invert the torta onto a serving platter, discarding the plastic wrap. Spread the top with the remaining Pesto and sprinkle with the remaining sun-dried tomatoes. Serves 18 to 22.

Mango Chutney Torta

1 cup 1% cottage cheese
16 ounces cream cheese, softened
1 teaspoon curry powder
1 cup dry roasted peanuts
1 cup chopped green onions
1 cup golden raisins

1 (9-ounce) jar mango chutney
1/2 cup chopped dry roasted
 peanuts
1/2 cup chopped green onions
3/4 cup shredded coconut, toasted

This recipe requires 8 hours of refrigeration. Line any shape loaf pan with plastic wrap, allowing enough overhang to cover the torta. Process the cottage cheese in a food processor until smooth, scraping the side of the bowl once. Add the cream cheese and curry powder and process until smooth. Add 1 cup peanuts, 1 cup green onions, the raisins and 1/4 cup of the chutney. Pulse three or four times or until the peanuts are coarsely chopped.

Spread half the cream cheese mixture in the prepared pan. Layer with 1/2 cup of the remaining chutney and the remaining cream cheese mixture. Spread with the remaining chutney. Chill, covered with plastic wrap, for 8 hours.

Invert the torta onto a serving platter, discarding the plastic wrap. Sprinkle 1/2 cup peanuts, 1/2 cup green onions and the coconut over and around the torta. Serve with assorted party crackers. Serves 25.

Photograph for this recipe on facing page.

My dining table has served four generations of my family on a sturdy mahogany back and strong yet graceful legs tipped with brass feet. During my great-grandmother's era, this table was used often and decorated in grand style with linen tablecloths and matching napkins, graced with silver candlesticks, and set with the best china, silverware, and crystal. My dining table even hosted my great-grandfather's weekly poker games many years ago. Over the years, as it has been passed down, the occasions have become less formal but no less important and special. It has continued its role of serving the family and hosting events. We now do not use the table on a daily basis, but always for special celebrations, all of the holidays, and bunco instead of poker. While I still use the monogrammed linen tablecloth that my mom used, the linen napkins have been replaced with paper napkins that correspond with the theme of the occasion. Some of the formality of the past has given way to an air of festivity and fun. I rather like it!
—D. Holbrook

Cremini Bouchées

1 (10×10-inch) sheet frozen puff
pastry, thawed
1 egg, lightly beaten
3 tablespoons unsalted butter
4 cups cremini, sliced

1/8 teaspoon salt
1/8 teaspoon pepper
1 tablespoon unsalted butter
3/4 cup chopped onion
1/8 teaspoon salt
1/8 teaspoon pepper

1/4 cup dry white wine
1/4 cup crème fraîche
2 tablespoons freshly grated
Parmesan cheese
2 teaspoons chopped fresh thyme

Cleaning Mushrooms

Cleaning mushrooms depends on their variety. White button mushrooms or cremini can be washed in a colander under cold running water. Once clean, trim the stem ends with a fresh cut. Use soon after as the mushrooms will continue to soak up water. More expensive mushrooms like chanterelle, morel, or even shiitake, should be gently wiped with a moist cloth. Most mushroom stems are edible, except for shiitake, which are tough, woody, and should be removed.

Preheat the oven to 400 degrees. Roll the pastry sheet 1/8 inch thick on a lightly floured hard surface. Trim the sides to form an 8-inch square. Cut into thirty-six squares. Arrange the squares in a single layer on a baking sheet lined with baking parchment. Brush the squares with the egg. Bake for 10 to 12 minutes or until golden brown. Remove to a wire rack to cool. Reduce the oven temperature to 350 degrees.

Heat 3 tablespoons butter in a sauté pan over medium heat. Add the mushrooms, 1/8 teaspoon salt and 1/8 teaspoon pepper. Sauté for 8 to 10 minutes or until the mushrooms begin to brown and become crisp. Remove to a bowl using a slotted spoon.

Wipe out the sauté pan with a paper towel. Heat 1 tablespoon butter in the sauté pan over medium heat until melted. Add the onion, 1/8 teaspoon salt and 1/8 teaspoon pepper. Cook for 6 minutes or until the onion is tender. Add the wine and cook for 4 to 5 minutes or until the wine is absorbed. Combine the mushrooms, onion, crème fraîche, cheese and thyme in a food processor. Pulse three or four times or until combined; do not purée.

Cut each pastry square crosswise into halves. Place 1/2 teaspoon of the mushroom mixture on half the pastry halves and top with the remaining pastry halves. Arrange on a baking sheet and bake for 5 minutes or until heated through. Serve warm.

The pastry may be baked 1 to 2 days in advance and stored, tightly covered with plastic wrap, at room temperature. The mushroom mixture may be prepared up to 2 days in advance and stored, covered, in the refrigerator. Assemble up to 3 hours in advance. Makes 3 dozen.

Chicken Satay with Spicy Peanut Sauce

Chicken Satay

1 cup rice wine vinegar
1 cup creamy peanut butter
1 cup soy sauce
1/4 cup vegetable oil
2 tablespoons chopped fresh ginger
1 1/2 tablespoons chopped cilantro
1 tablespoon sesame oil
1 1/2 pounds chicken, trimmed and
   cut into long strips

Peanut Sauce

1 cup creamy peanut butter
1/4 cup soy sauce
2 tablespoons brown sugar
2 tablespoons fresh lime juice
1 tablespoon sambal sauce
3/4 cup hot water
Chopped toasted peanuts
   (optional)
Sprig of cilantro (optional)

This recipe requires 3 hours of refrigeration. Preheat the oven to 350 degrees.

For the satay, combine the vinegar, peanut butter, soy sauce, vegetable oil, ginger, cilantro and sesame oil in a food processor and process until combined, or mix the ingredients in a bowl.

Skewer the chicken strips individually on 6-inch wooden skewers; do not bunch up the chicken strips on the skewers. Arrange the skewers in a shallow dish and pour the peanut butter mixture over the skewers, turning to coat. Marinate, covered, in the refrigerator for 3 hours or longer, turning occasionally.

Arrange the skewers in a single layer on a baking sheet lined with baking parchment. Bake for 10 to 12 minutes or until the chicken is cooked through, testing one skewer before removing from the oven.

For the sauce, combine the peanut butter, soy sauce, brown sugar, lime juice and sambal sauce in a food processor. Add the hot water gradually, processing constantly until of the desired consistency. Pour the sauce into a bowl. Sprinkle with peanuts and garnish with a sprig of cilantro. Serve with the satay. Makes 24 to 30 skewers.

Photograph for this recipe on page 80.

Toasting Nuts

Spread nuts evenly on a baking sheet and toast in a 375-degree oven for 5 to 8 minutes or until nicely browned. Stir midway through the baking process to prevent burning. Nuts can be drizzled with butter prior to toasting, if desired.

Duck Turnovers

1 duck, dressed
2 ribs celery, coarsely chopped
1 onion, coarsely chopped
Salt and black pepper to taste
1 egg
2 tablespoons milk
1/2 cup condensed cream of
   chicken soup

1/2 teaspoon salt
1/4 teaspoon white pepper
1/4 teaspoon thyme
1 tablespoon chopped roasted
   red bell pepper
2 refrigerator pie pastries

Preheat the oven to 350 degrees. Combine the duck, celery, onion and salt and black pepper to taste with enough water to cover in a stockpot. Bring to a simmer and simmer for about 30 minutes or until the duck is cooked through. Drain, reserving 1/2 cup of the broth and the vegetables. Chop the duck, discarding the bones. Process the duck and reserved vegetables in a food processor until ground, adding the reserved broth as needed to moisten.

Whisk the egg in a bowl until blended. Whisk 1 tablespoon of the egg with the milk in a bowl to make an egg wash. Combine the remaining egg, 1 cup of the ground duck mixture, the soup, 1/2 teaspoon salt, 1/4 teaspoon white pepper, the thyme and roasted pepper in a bowl and mix well.

Roll the pastries on a lightly floured surface and cut into 3-inch rounds using a cutter. Spoon 1 slightly rounded tablespoon of the duck filling onto half of each round. Moisten the pastry edges with water and fold over to enclose the filling. Press the edges with a fork dipped in the egg wash. Brush the tops with the remaining egg wash.

Arrange the turnovers in a single layer on a greased baking sheet. Bake for 20 to 25 minutes or until light brown. Serve with pomegranate or raspberry chipotle sauce, hot mustard, sweet-and-sour sauce or the sauce of your choice. The turnovers may be frozen for future use. Complete the recipe up to the egg wash and arrange the turnovers on a baking sheet. Freeze until firm. Wrap the frozen turnovers in foil and place in a sealable plastic freezer bag. Store for up to 6 months in the freezer. Serves 12.

Photograph for this recipe on page 75.

Savory Prosciutto and Fig Tartlets

1 cup dried figs or apricots
1 sheet frozen puff pastry
1 (4- to 6-ounce) package
    crumbled goat cheese

1 (3- to 4-ounce) package sliced
    prosciutto
Salt and freshly cracked pepper
    to taste

Apricot preserves (optional)

Preheat the oven to 400 degrees. Soak the figs with enough water to cover in a bowl for 30 minutes. Drain, pat dry and finely chop. Unwrap the puff pastry on a lightly floured surface. Thaw for 15 minutes.

Cut the pastry into 1-inch squares. Arrange the squares on an ungreased baking sheet. Bake for 10 to 15 minutes or until light brown. Maintain the oven temperature.

Top each pastry square with 1 teaspoon of the goat cheese and 1 teaspoon of the figs. Roll the prosciutto slices into small logs and arrange over the prepared layers. Secure with wooden picks previously soaked in water. Bake just until the cheese melts and the tartlets are warm. Serve hot. These tartlets are better served hot, so heat as needed. Top with a dollop of apricot preserves. Serves 10.

Photograph for this recipe on page 74.

Crab Rangoon

16 ounces cream cheese, softened
3 green onions, finely chopped
2 teaspoons minced garlic
1 1/2 pounds crab meat, drained
    and shells removed

1 teaspoon Worcestershire sauce
1 package won ton wrappers
Vegetable oil

Beat the cream cheese, green onions and garlic in a mixing bowl until combined. Fold in the crab meat and Worcestershire sauce. Spoon 1/2 to 1 teaspoon of the crab meat filling on each won ton wrapper. Moisten the edges with water and fold over to enclose the filling forming triangles; seal the edges.

Fry in hot oil in a deep-fat fryer until golden brown; be careful not to overcook as the cream cheese will melt. Drain on paper towels. Makes 32.

Fried Green Tomatoes with Crab Meat Rémoulade

Crab Meat Rémoulade

1 1/2 cups mayonnaise

1/4 cup chopped onion

2 tablespoons finely chopped green onions

2 tablespoons chopped flat-leaf parsley

2 tablespoons fresh lemon juice

2 teaspoons Creole mustard

Salt and freshly ground pepper to taste

Hot sauce to taste

1 pound lump crab meat, drained and shells removed

Fried Green Tomatoes

2 pounds green tomatoes, trimmed and cut into 1/2-inch slices

Salt and freshly ground pepper to taste

3/4 cup vegetable oil

1 1/4 cups all-purpose flour

3/4 cup yellow cornmeal

3/4 cup buttermilk

2 eggs, lightly beaten

4 cups baby salad greens

For the rémoulade, combine the mayonnaise, onion, green onions, parsley, lemon juice and Creole mustard in a bowl and mix well. Season with salt, pepper and hot sauce. Fold in the crab meat until coated. Chill, covered, in the refrigerator.

For the tomatoes, season the tomato slices with salt and pepper. Heat the oil in a large skillet over medium heat. Pour the flour into a shallow dish. Pour the cornmeal into a shallow dish. Whisk the buttermilk and eggs in a bowl until blended.

Coat the tomato slices with the flour, shaking off any excess. Dip in the buttermilk mixture and then coat with the cornmeal, shaking off any excess. Fry the slices three or four at a time in the hot oil for 2 minutes per side or until golden brown. Drain on paper towels.

Mound equals portions of the salad greens in the center of six serving plates. Top equally with the fried tomatoes and the rémoulade. Serve immediately. Serves 6.

My kitchen table holds fond memories of great family recipes that have been passed on from generation to generation and enjoyed there. I've heard, "the kitchen is the heart of the home and the table is the foundation from which the memories are made." We love to play dominoes after holiday dinners, and if those tables could talk they would tell you the girls always beat the boys fair and square. Of course, the boys would say, "The girls won because they cheated." Only the girls and the table know the truth!   —A. Mason

Vietnamese Spring Rolls

1 cup thin rice noodles
15 large shrimp, cooked, peeled
   and deveined
2 cups julienned green cabbage
1/2 cup bean sprouts
1/4 cup julienned carrots

5 green onions, chopped
1 tablespoon lime juice
1 tablespoon soy sauce
1 1/2 teaspoons grated fresh ginger
   (optional)
1 package spring roll wrappers

1/4 cup fresh cilantro, basil or
   mint leaves
1/2 cup sweet chili dipping sauce or
   peanut sauce

Cook the noodles using the package directions; drain. Cut the shrimp into halves along the vein lines. Toss the noodles, cabbage, bean sprouts, carrots, green onions, lime juice, soy sauce and ginger in a bowl until combined.

Immerse the wrappers in cold water in a bowl for 15 seconds or until pliable. Place about 2 tablespoons of the noodle mixture on each wrapper. Arrange two shrimp halves and some of the cilantro leaves on each wrapper and roll like a burrito. Serve immediately with the chili dipping sauce. Cover the spring rolls with a damp towel to prevent drying out if not served immediately. Makes 15.

Photograph for this recipe on page 80.

Cabbage

Cabbage is primarily a Texas winter vegetable, but a small to moderate harvest takes place year-round. Growers harvest more than 9,000 acres, most of it planted in green cabbage known for heavy density and high quality. Texas also produces Chinese or napa cabbage, red cabbage, and savoy cabbage.

Spicy Pretzels

1 1/2 pounds pretzel sticks or
   nuggets
1 teaspoon cayenne pepper

1 teaspoon onion powder
1 teaspoon garlic powder

1 envelope ranch salad
   dressing mix
1 cup canola oil

Place the pretzels in a very large bowl. Sprinkle the cayenne pepper, onion powder, garlic powder and dressing mix over the pretzels. Add the canola oil and stir until combined.

Let stand for 15 minutes and stir to coat. Let stand for 45 to 60 minutes longer, stirring every 15 minutes until the oil and spices are absorbed. Store in sealable plastic bags or airtight containers. Serves 10 to 12.

The Sideboard

Sides are the table's unsung heroes. These versatile dishes of vegetables or grains prepared with spices and herbs and cooked to perfection are used to complement the meal, beautify our plates, and fill our tabletops with variety. Side dishes are as diverse as the personalities of the people we serve. When coupled together with care, an array of side dishes can constitute an entire meal or add a unique and interesting flare to a simple entrée. A variety of side dishes offered to family and guests can satisfy any number of differing tastes of those around any table.

"The greatest delight the fields and woods minister is the suggestion of an occult relation between man and the vegetable. 'I am not alone and unacknowledged.' They nod to me and I to them."

—Ralph Waldo Emerson

Walnut Cranberry Slaw

2 cups chopped or shredded
green cabbage
2 cups chopped or shredded
red cabbage

1 cup walnuts
1 cup dried cranberries
1/2 cup sliced purple onion
1/2 cup chopped red bell pepper
1/2 cup vegetable oil

1/3 cup cider vinegar
1/3 cup sugar
1 teaspoon celery seeds
1/2 teaspoon salt

This recipe requires 4 hours of refrigeration. Toss the cabbage, walnuts, cranberries, onion and bell pepper together in a bowl. Whisk the oil, vinegar, sugar, celery seeds and salt in a bowl until the sugar dissolves. Drizzle over the cabbage mixture. Chill, covered, for 4 hours. Drain before serving. Serves 12.

Photograph for this recipe on facing page.

Baked Potato Salad

2 pounds small red potatoes,
cut into halves
1/4 cup canola oil
2 teaspoons kosher salt

8 ounces bacon, chopped and
crisp-cooked
1 cup sour cream
8 ounces sharp Cheddar
cheese, shredded

1 bunch scallions, chopped
1/2 cup (1 stick) butter, cubed
2 tablespoons cracked pepper
2 teaspoons kosher salt

If your recipe calls for a mayonnaise dressing, new or waxy potatoes are best. Warm dressings and vinaigrettes, however, are better absorbed by more mealy potatoes such as Idaho.

Preheat the oven to 350 degrees. Toss the potatoes with the canola oil and 2 teaspoons salt in a bowl until coated. Arrange the potatoes in a single layer on a baking sheet. Bake for 30 minutes or until the potatoes are tender. Cool slightly and cut the potatoes into large chunks.

Combine the potatoes, bacon, sour cream, cheese, scallions and butter in a large bowl and toss gently, being careful to leave the potatoes in large chunks. Season with the pepper and 2 teaspoons salt. Serves 8.

Courtesty of Kent Rathbun, Executive Chef/Partner, Jasper's

Crispy Fried Asparagus

18 thick asparagus spears
Coarse salt to taste
1/2 cup canola oil

1 cup panko
   (Japanese bread crumbs)
Freshly ground pepper to taste
2 eggs

*P*repare an ice bath by filling a large bowl with ice and water. Line two large plates with paper towels. Snap off the woody ends of the asparagus. Bring a large saucepan of salted water to a boil over high heat. Add the asparagus and boil for 4 to 5 minutes or just until tender. Drain the asparagus in a colander and place in the ice bath to stop the cooking process; drain and pat dry.

Heat the canola oil in a shallow skillet over medium-high heat until shimmering. Mix the bread crumbs, salt and pepper in a shallow dish. Whisk the eggs in a shallow bowl until blended.

Dip the asparagus in the eggs and then coat in the bread crumbs. Fry the asparagus in batches in the hot oil for 3 to 5 minutes or until golden brown. Serve immediately. Serves 4.

Roasted Brussels Sprouts with Pecans

2 pounds fresh brussels sprouts,
   cut into halves
1 cup chopped pecans
2 tablespoons olive oil
2 garlic cloves, chopped

1 teaspoon kosher salt
1 teaspoon pepper
4 to 6 slices bacon, crisp-cooked
   and crumbled

*P*reheat the oven to 400 degrees. Toss the brussels sprouts, pecans, olive oil, garlic, salt and pepper in a large bowl. Spread on a baking sheet. Roast for 20 to 30 minutes or until the brussels sprouts are golden brown and tender, stirring occasionally. Sprinkle with the bacon prior to serving. Serves 8.

Photograph for this recipe on facing page.

Rockin' Green Beans

1 teaspoon salt
1 pound green beans or haricots
    verts, tips cut off
6 to 8 cups water

2/3 cup chopped onion
6 tablespoons butter
1/3 cup chopped
    crisp-cooked bacon

1/3 cup packed brown sugar
1 tablespoon Worcestershire sauce
1/2 teaspoon pepper
1/4 teaspoon salt

Bring the water and 1 teaspoon salt to a boil in a saucepan. Blanche the beans in the boiling water for 4 to 5 minutes or until al dente. Drain and immediately plunge the beans into an ice bath to stop the cooking process; drain again.

Sauté the onion in the butter in a saucepan until tender. Stir in the bacon, brown sugar, Worcestershire sauce, pepper and 1/4 teaspoon salt. Simmer for 1 minute. Mix in the beans and simmer for 2 to 3 minutes or until heated through. Serve immediately. Serves 4.

Photograph for this recipe on page 147.

Spicy Sautéed Broccolini with Garlic

1 pound broccolini, trimmed
Salt to taste
1 tablespoon olive oil
3 garlic cloves, minced

1/2 teaspoon hot red pepper flakes
1/2 cup chicken stock or broth
Freshly cracked pepper

Cook the broccolini in boiling salted water in a saucepan for 5 minutes or until the stems are tender-crisp; drain. Immediately plunge the broccolini into an ice bath to stop the cooking process. Drain and pat dry.

Heat the olive oil in a large sauté pan over medium heat until hot but not smoking. Add the garlic and red pepper flakes and sauté for 2 minutes. Stir in the stock and simmer for 3 minutes. Add the broccolini and sauté for 2 minutes. Remove the broccolini to a serving bowl and sprinkle lightly with salt and freshly cracked pepper. Serves 4.

Carrot Soufflé

1 pound carrots, cooked
1/2 cup sugar
1/2 cup (1 stick) margarine, melted
3 eggs
3 tablespoons all-purpose flour

1 teaspoon baking powder
1 teaspoon vanilla extract
Dash of cinnamon
1/4 cup chopped pecans or nuts
   of choice

1/4 cup crushed cornflakes
3 tablespoons brown sugar
2 tablespoons margarine, melted
Dash of cinnamon

Preheat the oven to 350 degrees. Place the carrots in a food processor and pulse. Add the sugar, 1/2 cup margarine, the eggs, flour, baking powder, vanilla and a dash of cinnamon and pulse until blended. Spoon the carrot mixture into a lightly greased 1 1/2- quart baking dish.

Mix the pecans, cornflakes, brown sugar, 2 tablespoons margarine and a dash of cinnamon in a bowl. Sprinkle over the carrot mixture. Bake for 35 to 45 minutes or until light brown. Substitute sweet potatoes for the carrots for a totally different flavor. Serves 4 to 6.

Photograph for this recipe on page 103.

Bourbon Cream Corn

1/4 cup (1/2 stick) butter
4 garlic cloves, minced
4 shallots, minced
3 cups fresh corn kernels
1/4 cup chopped red bell pepper

1/4 cup bourbon
1 cup heavy cream
1/4 cup chopped scallions
1 tablespoon kosher salt
1 tablespoon cracked pepper

Melt the butter in a large sauté pan. Sauté the garlic and shallots in the butter until translucent. Stir in the corn and bell pepper and cook for 2 minutes. Deglaze the pan with the bourbon and stir in the cream.

Cook until the mixture begins to thicken, stirring occasionally. Mix in the scallions, salt and pepper. Spoon into a serving bowl. Serves 8.

Courtesy of Kent Rathbun, Executive Chef/Partner, Jasper's

Edamame Succotash

4 slices bacon
1 onion, chopped
2 tablespoons extra-virgin olive oil
   (optional)

1 red bell pepper, chopped
12 ounces frozen corn kernels
2 cups frozen edamame
2 pinches of sea salt

2 pinches freshly ground pepper
1/4 cup heavy cream
Salt and pepper to taste

Cook the bacon in a cast-iron skillet until brown and crisp. Remove the bacon to a platter, reserving the bacon drippings. Sauté the onion in the reserved bacon drippings for 4 minutes or wipe the skillet with a paper towel and sauté the onion in the olive oil for 4 minutes. Stir in the bell pepper, corn, beans, 2 pinches salt and 2 pinches pepper. Cook for 20 minutes. Stir in the cream and cook for 5 minutes, stirring occasionally. Season with salt and pepper to taste. Spoon the succotash into a serving bowl and crumble the bacon over the top. Serves 6 to 8.

Photograph for this recipe on facing page.

Eggplant and Feta Cheese Rolls

2 globe eggplants
   (about 1 1/2 pounds)
Extra-virgin olive oil for brushing
   and drizzling
Salt and pepper to taste

1 1/2 cups crumbled feta cheese
2 tablespoons extra-virgin olive oil
Grated zest of 1 lemon
2 tablespoons chopped fresh
   flat-leaf parsley

1 teaspoon fresh thyme leaves
Fresh lemon juice to taste
1 red onion, chopped (optional)
1 green onion, chopped (optional)

Preheat a charcoal fire on medium or preheat a gas grill to 350 degrees. Brush the grill racks with oil. Cut the eggplant lengthwise into 1/4-inch slices. Brush both sides with olive oil and sprinkle with salt and pepper. Grill for 4 to 5 minutes per side or until softened and golden brown. Remove from the heat and place the slices in a paper bag or sealed container. Let cool for 20 minutes or until room temperature. Toss the cheese, 2 tablespoons olive oil, the lemon zest, parsley and thyme together in a bowl. Place about 2 teaspoons of the cheese mixture along the short edge of each eggplant slice and roll tightly to enclose the filling. Secure with moistened wooden picks, if desired. Arrange the rolls seam side down on a serving platter or on individual serving plates. Drizzle with olive oil and lemon juice. Garnish with the red onion and green onion. Serve at room temperature. Serves 6.

Photograph for this recipe on page 103.

Texas "1015" Onion Straws

5 to 7 cups vegetable oil
1 large Texas 1015 onion
2 cups buttermilk

2 cups all-purpose flour
1 1/2 teaspoons Creole seasoning
3 poblano peppers, thinly sliced

Heat the oil in a deep-fat fryer to 360 degrees. Cut the onion into 1/8-inch-thick slices. Soak the onion in the buttermilk in a bowl for 5 minutes; drain.

Mix the flour and Creole seasoning in a shallow dish. Coat the onion and poblano chiles with the seasoned flour. Fry the onion and poblano peppers in the hot oil until golden brown and crisp; drain. Serve immediately. Serves 4.

Photograph for this recipe on page 187.

Photograph for this recipe on page 187.

Onions

Texas produces the year's first domestic crop of mild, sweet spring onions. The famous Texas 1015 appears on the market in April and May. These extra-large Grano onions with light brown skin and predominantly single centers are an attractive product for retail shoppers and the hotel-restaurant industry.

Wild Rice with Almonds and Dried Cherries

1 tablespoon olive oil
1/2 cup finely chopped carrots
1/2 cup finely chopped celery
3/4 cup finely chopped onion
1 cup wild rice
4 to 4 1/2 cups chicken broth
1 cup shiitake mushrooms, sliced
   (optional)

1 teaspoon chopped flat-leaf
   parsley
1/2 cup dried cherries
1/2 cup almonds, sliced
   and blanched
1 tablespoon butter
1/2 teaspoon kosher salt
1/4 teaspoon freshly cracked pepper

Heat the olive oil in a stockpot over medium heat. Add the carrots, celery and onion. Sauté for 5 minutes or until the onion is translucent. Add the wild rice and stir to coat with the olive oil. Add the broth. Cook for about 1 hour and 10 minutes or until the wild rice is tender, curled and split. Add the mushrooms and cook for 10 minutes; remove from the heat. Stir in the parsley, dried cherries and almonds. Season with the butter, salt and pepper. Serves 6.

Baked Portobello Mushrooms with Goat Cheese

Marinara Sauce

1/2 small onion, chopped

2 tablespoons olive oil

4 garlic cloves, minced

1 teaspoon crushed red
  pepper flakes

1 (29-ounce) can crushed
  tomatoes

1 (15-ounce) can diced tomatoes

1/4 cup red wine

1/4 cup chopped fresh basil, or
  1 tablespoon dried basil

1 teaspoon dried oregano

Baked Portobello Mushroom

4 large portobello mushrooms,
  stems and gills removed

10 ounces fresh spinach, chopped

1 tablespoon olive oil

4 ounces goat cheese, crumbled

2 tablespoons pine nuts

1 tablespoon chopped fresh basil

Preheat the oven to 375 degrees.

For the sauce, sauté the onion in the olive oil in a saucepan for 3 minutes. Add the garlic and red pepper flakes and sauté for 1 minute. Stir in the tomatoes, wine, basil and oregano. Simmer for 20 minutes or longer, stirring occasionally.

For the mushrooms, spread 2 cups of the marinara sauce in a 9×9-inch baking dish. Arrange the mushroom caps stem side up over the sauce. Sauté the spinach in the olive oil and spoon onto the mushrooms. Top evenly with the goat cheese and pine nuts.

Bake for 30 minutes and sprinkle with the basil. Serve immediately with baguette slices or any good-quality bread torn into pieces for dipping. Serves 4.

Photograph for this recipe on page 103.

Spinach

Texas produces good-quality spinach with clean, fresh, crisp leaves and good green coloring. Smooth-leaf varieties suitable for processing comprise about 70 percent of the crop. Fresh market crinkle-leaf Savoy makes up the remainder. A cool weather crop, spinach is harvested primarily from late fall through early spring.

Jalapeño Cheddar Gratin Potatoes

2¹/₂ pounds russet potatoes,
   cleaned and peeled
1¹/₂ cups heavy cream
1 egg
2 jalapeño peppers, minced
1 teaspoon minced fresh thyme
1 teaspoon minced fresh basil

¹/₄ teaspoon salt
¹/₄ teaspoon pepper
¹/₂ cup (2 ounces) shredded
   Cheddar cheese
¹/₂ cup (2 ounces) shredded
   Monterey Jack cheese

Preheat the oven to 425 degrees. Cut the potatoes into ¹/₈-inch-thick slices. Combine the potatoes, cream, egg, one of the jalapeño peppers, thyme, basil, salt and pepper in a bowl and mix well.

Spoon half the potato mixture into an 8×8-inch baking dish. Sprinkle with half the Cheddar cheese, half the Monterey Jack cheese and the remaining jalapeño peppers. Layer with the remaining potato mixture, remaining Cheddar cheese and remaining Monterey Jack cheese.

Bake for 1 hour or until the potatoes are tender, covering with foil to prevent overbrowning. Add additional cheese for a cheesier flavor. You may substitute Gruyère cheese for the Cheddar cheese and green onions for the jalapeño peppers. Serves 4.

Photograph for this recipe on facing page.

Gratin Pans

All gratin pans have two common factors: they are shallow and ovenproof. This provides maximum surface area for the ingredients in a gratin dish to broil evenly and ensure that each serving has been browned or broiled. "Au gratin" refers to any dish prepared with cheese and bread crumbs, topped with butter, and heated or broiled in the oven or on the grill.

There is a farm in Central Texas that has been in my husband's family for more than one hundred years. My husband's grandfather was born in the farmhouse. Many years later, my husband went there as a boy to visit his grandparents. As long as he can remember, there was a lazy Susan–style dining table with milk paint in the kitchen. When my husband and I married, his grandmother gave us the table for us to refinish and use in our own home. Today, the farm is still in the family, owned by my husband's uncle and cousins. Over the years, the old farmhouse has deteriorated and is no longer in use, though it has been declared a Texas Historical Marker. We still have the old table and treasure it for its history. It holds many memories of crafting, dinners, and long conversations. —L. Earle

Make-Ahead Creamy Mashed Potatoes

10 potatoes (Yukon gold
    potatoes preferred)
8 garlic cloves
2 to 3 tablespoons olive oil
10 slices bacon, crisp-cooked
    and crumbled
1 cup sour cream
1/2 to 3/4 cup milk
1/2 cup (1 stick) butter, melted

1/2 cup (2 ounces) shredded
    Cheddar cheese
3 ounces cream cheese, softened
1/2 cup thinly sliced green onions
2 teaspoons onion powder
2 teaspoons salt
1 teaspoon pepper
1/2 cup (2 ounces) shredded
    Cheddar cheese

Preheat the oven to 350 degrees. Combine the potatoes with enough water to cover in a large saucepan and bring to a boil over medium-high heat. Reduce the heat to medium. Cook for 10 to 15 minutes or until the potatoes are tender; drain.

Place the garlic cloves on a sheet of foil large enough to enclose and drizzle with the olive oil. Seal tightly. Roast for 15 to 20 minutes or until the garlic is soft and creamy.

Combine the potatoes, bacon, sour cream, milk, butter, 1/2 cup Cheddar cheese, the cream cheese, green onions, onion powder, salt and pepper in a mixing bowl. Beat until creamy. Spread the potato mixture in a lightly greased baking dish and sprinkle with 1/2 cup Cheddar cheese. Cover with plastic wrap and chill until ready to bake.

Let stand at room temperature for 30 minutes and remove the plastic wrap. Bake for 45 minutes or until heated through. Serves 10 to 12.

Photograph for this recipe on page 156.

Potatoes

Russet, yellow, and red potatoes are grown in Texas, with about half on the High Plains and the rest in the Winter Garden area and Rio Grande Valley. Seventy percent are sold fresh, while 30 percent are processed into potato chips. Texas sweet potatoes are produced in North East Texas and are sold throughout the United States. These oblong sweet potatoes have a bright color and smooth skins that are perfect for any occasion.

Creamed Spinach

2 (10-ounce) packages frozen
chopped spinach
1/4 cup (1/2 stick) butter
3 tablespoons all-purpose flour
1/4 cup chopped onion
1 teaspoon minced garlic

1/2 teaspoon each salt and pepper
1/8 teaspoon nutmeg
1/2 cup (2 ounces) grated
Parmesan cheese
1/2 cup (2 ounces) shredded
Pepper Jack cheese

1 cup half-and-half
1/2 cup (2 ounces) grated
Parmesan cheese
3 slices bacon, crisp-cooked
and crumbled

Cook the spinach using the package directions. Drain the spinach over a bowl and press the spinach to release any remaining moisture. Reserve 1/2 cup of the spinach liquid. Melt the butter in a saucepan and stir in the flour. Cook until smooth, stirring constantly. Add the onion and the reserved 1/2 cup spinach liquid and mix well. Cook for 5 minutes or until the onion is tender, stirring occasionally. Stir in the garlic, salt, pepper and nutmeg. Add 1/2 cup Parmesan cheese and the Pepper Jack cheese. Cook until the cheese melts, stirring constantly. Stir in the half-and-half and fold in the spinach. Cook just until heated through, stirring frequently. Spoon the spinach mixture into a serving bowl and sprinkle with 1/2 cup Parmesan cheese and the bacon. Serve immediately. Serves 6 to 8.

> You may spoon the spinach mixture into a 2-quart baking dish and sprinkle with 1/2 cup Parmesan cheese and the bacon. Bake in a preheated 300-degree oven for 15 minutes or until bubbly.

Sautéed Sugar Snap Peas

1 pound sugar snap peas,
strings removed
8 ounces carrots, peeled and
cut into matchsticks
Salt to taste

1 bunch radishes, cut into
1/4-inch slices
2 tablespoons olive oil
1/4 teaspoon freshly
cracked pepper
1 tablespoon rice wine vinegar

1 teaspoon cider vinegar
2 to 4 tablespoons white
sesame seeds
1 red bell pepper, roasted, peeled
and chopped (optional)

Blanch the peas and carrots in boiling salted water in a saucepan for 1 minute; the vegetables should still be bright in color. Drain and immediately plunge the vegetables into a bowl of ice water to stop the cooking process; drain. Sauté the radishes in the olive oil in a skillet for 1 minute or until tender. Stir in the peas and carrots and sauté for 1 minute. Stir in the pepper, rice wine vinegar and cider vinegar. Season with salt. Mix in the sesame seeds and bell pepper. Serves 4.

Photograph for this recipe on page 103.

Roasted Butternut Squash with Apples

3 cups chopped peeled seeded
    butternut squash (1-inch cubes)
1 tablespoon olive oil
1 teaspoon kosher salt

1/2 teaspoon nutmeg
1/4 teaspoon freshly
    cracked pepper
2 cups chopped peeled Granny
    Smith apples (1-inch cubes)

1 tablespoon olive oil
1/4 cup currants
1/4 cup maple syrup
2 tablespoons butter
1 1/2 tablespoons lemon juice

Preheat the oven to 350 degrees. Toss the squash with 1 tablespoon olive oil, the salt, nutmeg and pepper in a baking pan. Roast for 30 minutes, stirring several times. Maintain the oven temperature. Toss the apples with 1 tablespoon olive oil in a baking pan. Roast for about 15 minutes. Maintain the oven temperature. Combine the squash, apples, currants, maple syrup, butter and lemon juice in a bowl and mix gently. Spread the squash mixture in a baking pan. Roast for about 10 to 15 minutes; the vegetables should not be mushy. Serves 6.

Photograph for this recipe on page 102.

Plat de Courgettes

2 pounds zucchini, cut into
    1/4-inch rounds
1 (29-ounce) can whole
    tomatoes, drained
2 teaspoons garlic powder

2 tablespoons butter
2 tablespoons all-purpose flour
1/2 teaspoon salt
1/2 teaspoon pepper
1 cup milk

6 ounces Swiss cheese, shredded
1/2 cup panko
    (Japanese bread crumbs)
1 teaspoon parsley
2 tablespoons butter

Preheat the oven to 350 degrees. Steam the zucchini in a steamer for 10 minutes or until tender. Drain and pat dry. Arrange the zucchini in a buttered baking dish. Squeeze any remaining juice from the tomatoes using your hand. Tear open each tomato and arrange over the zucchini. Sprinkle with the garlic powder. Melt 2 tablespoons butter in a saucepan. Stir in the flour, salt and pepper until blended. Cook until thickened. Add the milk gradually, stirring constantly. Cook until a thick and creamy white sauce forms. Add the cheese gradually and cook until the cheese melts. Pour the sauce over the prepared layers. Sprinkle with a mixture of the bread crumbs and parsley and dot with 2 tablespoons butter. Bake for 45 to 50 minutes or until light brown. Serves 8.

Photograph for this recipe on page 103.

Polenta with Mushroom Ragout

1 cup instant polenta
Salt and freshly cracked pepper
   to taste
4 ounces boursin cheese
Grated zest of 1/2 lemon

1/2 cup walnut pieces, chopped
3 tablespoons butter
1 1/2 pounds cremini, stemmed and
   thinly sliced
2 garlic cloves, crushed
1/2 cup chicken stock

1 teaspoon cornstarch
3 tablespoons chopped fresh basil
2 tablespoons lemon juice
1/2 teaspoon salt

Preheat the oven to the broiler setting. Line a 12-inch baking pan with baking parchment. Cook the polenta using the package directions. Season to taste with salt and pepper and remove from the heat. Add the cheese and lemon zest and stir until the cheese melts. Spread the polenta evenly in the prepared pan with a rubber spatula. Let cool for 40 minutes or until firm. You may prepare to this point up to 1 day in advance. Store, covered, in the refrigerator.

Toast the walnuts in a small skillet over medium heat for 3 to 4 minutes or until they begin to brown and become fragrant, shaking the skillet occasionally. Remove to a plate to cool.

Melt the butter in a sauté pan and add the mushrooms and garlic. Cook for about 5 minutes or until the mushrooms are soft and start to release their juices. Whisk the stock and cornstarch together in a small bowl until blended and stir into the mushroom mixture. Stir in the basil, lemon juice, 1/2 teaspoon salt and pepper. Cook for 3 to 4 minutes or until the mushrooms are tender and the sauce is slightly thickened.

Cut the polenta into shapes with a cookie cutter of choice and place on a buttered baking sheet. Broil 4 to 6 inches from the heat source for about 5 minutes or until light brown. Arrange the polenta on a serving platter and top with the mushroom ragout. Sprinkle with the walnuts. Serve immediately. Serves 5 to 6.

Photograph for this recipe on page 103.

Clancy's Crawfish Corn Bread

2 teaspoons butter or shortening
2 cups cornmeal
2 tablespoons Creole seasoning
1 teaspoon salt
1 teaspoon baking soda
2 large onions, chopped
3 tablespoons finely chopped
   jalapeño chiles

2 tablespoons chopped garlic
2 tablespoons extra-virgin olive oil
3 eggs
3 egg yolks
3 (15-ounce) cans
   cream-style corn
1 (15-ounce) can whole kernel
   corn, drained

16 ounces mild Cheddar
   cheese, shredded
2 tablespoons flat-leaf
   parsley, chopped
1/4 cup vegetable oil
2 pounds fresh crawfish tails, or
   3 (12-ounce) packages crawfish
   tails, cleaned and drained

Preheat the oven to 375 degrees. Coat two cast-iron skillets with the butter. Mix the cornmeal, Creole seasoning, salt and baking soda in a bowl. Sauté the onions, jalapeño chiles and garlic in the olive oil in a skillet until the onions are tender.

Whisk the eggs and egg yolks in a bowl until blended. Stir in the corn, cheese, parsley and vegetable oil. Mix in the cornmeal mixture. Fold in the onion mixture. Add the crawfish and mix well.

Spoon the crawfish mixture evenly into the prepared pans. Bake for 60 to 75 minutes or until light brown. Cut into squares and serve warm. Omit the crawfish, if desired, or add pickled jalapeño chiles for more heat. Serves 16.

Photograph for this recipe on facing page.

My dining table is one I acquired when I married my husband. He purchased the table from a secondhand store years before we met and used it as a desk. Its simplistic nature provided a great work surface for several years before I reclaimed it for its original purpose—to share moments with friends and family over home-cooked goodness. The table now bears evidence of us joining our lives together as it shows signs of wear. There are even claw marks from our Labradors the time they tried to join us at the table for dinner and conversation. We look forward to the character it will continue to develop as our family grows over the years.
—K. Sanders

Lobster Macaroni and Cheese with Truffle Oil

1/4 cup olive oil
1 1/2 pounds lobster meat, chopped
1/4 cup extra-virgin olive oil
32 ounces orzo
2 tablespoons minced garlic
2 tablespoons minced shallots

8 cups chicken stock, strained
2 cups heavy cream
1 cup (4 ounces) grated
    Romano cheese
2 tablespoons basil leaves,
    chiffonade
2 tablespoons spinach leaves,
    chiffonade

2 tablespoons chopped oregano
2 tablespoons chopped parsley
8 ounces prosciutto, julienned
2 tablespoons cracked pepper
2 tablespoon kosher salt
2 tablespoons truffle oil

Heat 1/4 cup olive oil in a large stockpot over medium to high heat and add the lobster meat. Sauté for about 2 minutes or until the lobster meat is medium-rare. Remove the lobster meat to a platter using a slotted spoon, reserving the pan drippings. Add 1/4 cup extra-virgin olive oil to the reserved pan drippings. Reduce the heat to medium and add half the pasta.

Sauté until the pasta is golden brown. Stir in the remaining pasta, the garlic, shallots and 4 cups of the stock. Cook until the pasta absorbs most of the stock, stirring occasionally. Add the remaining 4 cups stock and cook until all of the stock is absorbed. Add the cream and cheese and cook until the cheese melts, stirring constantly. Stir in the basil, spinach, oregano and parsley.

Sauté the prosciutto in a sauté pan until crisp. Add to the pasta mixture and mix well. Stir in the lobster meat, pepper, salt and truffle oil. Serves 8.

Courtesy of Kent Rathbun, Executive Chef/Partner, Jasper's

"Kitchen Sink" Orzo

10 ounces orzo (about 1 1/2 cups)
2 teaspoons olive oil
1 head radicchio, finely chopped
(about 1 cup)
1/3 cup oil-pack sun-dried
tomatoes, drained and chopped

6 tablespoons olive oil
1/4 to 1/2 cup kalamata
olives, sliced
1/4 cup balsamic vinegar
1 garlic clove, chopped
1/2 cup fresh basil, chiffonade

1/2 cup (2 ounces) grated good-
quality Parmesan cheese
1/2 cup pine nuts, toasted
1 teaspoon kosher salt
1 teaspoon freshly ground pepper

Cook the pasta using the package directions until al dente; drain. Toss the pasta with 2 teaspoons olive oil in a bowl until coated. Let stand until cool.

Toss the radicchio, sun-dried tomatoes, 6 tablespoons olive oil, the olives, vinegar and garlic in a bowl until combined. Add the tomato mixture to the cooled pasta and mix well. Stir in the basil, cheese and pine nuts. Season with the salt and pepper. Serves 12.

Israeli Couscous

16 ounces Israeli couscous
2 tablespoons olive oil
1 pint red teardrop tomatoes
1 yellow bell pepper,
cut into matchsticks
1/2 cup loosely packed fresh
basil, chiffonade

1/2 cup chopped oil-pack sun-dried
tomatoes, drained
1/2 cup kalamata olives,
cut into quarters
3/4 cup olive oil
1 small shallot, minced
3 tablespoons fresh lemon juice

3 tablespoons balsamic vinegar
1 tablespoon red wine vinegar
Salt and pepper to taste

Prepare the couscous using the package directions. Toss the couscous with 2 tablespoons olive oil, the teardrop tomatoes, bell pepper, basil, sun-dried tomatoes and olives in a bowl. Combine 3/4 cup olive oil, the shallot, lemon juice, balsamic vinegar, wine vinegar, salt and pepper in a jar with a tight-fitting lid and seal tightly. Shake to mix. Add the desired amount of the vinaigrette to the couscous mixture and mix well. Serve with Boursin-Stuffed Veal Chops (page 146). Serves 4.

Photograph for this recipe on page 147.

The Dining Table

The concept of eating together while assembled at dining room tables originated during medieval times. Dining tables would usually offer an abundance of foods. In Southeast Texas, dining together and generously sharing our bounty is a time-honored tradition. As the modern family evolves, moments at the table become less frequent and more precious, encouraging us to plan special time with family over an evening meal. The dinner table has become a fixture that symbolizes trust, warmth, and love, even before any food is served.

"Enchant, stay beautiful and graceful, but do this, eat well.
Bring the same consideration to the preparation of your food as you devote to your appearance.
Let your dinner be a poem, like your dress."

—Charles Pierre Monselet

Beef Wellington

2 tablespoons olive oil
1 shallot, chopped
12 ounces white
    mushrooms, chopped
1/2 cup white wine
1 tablespoon chopped
    flat-leaf parsley

Salt and pepper to taste
1 (2- to 4-pound) beef tenderloin
1 sheet (or more) frozen puff
    pastry, thawed
1 egg yolk, lightly beaten

Preheat the oven to 350 degrees. Heat a sauté pan until hot and pour in the olive oil. Sauté the shallot in the hot oil until translucent. Add the mushrooms and cook until all the liquid evaporates. Stir in the wine and parsley and cook until the wine evaporates. Season with salt and pepper.

Trim the tenderloin of all fat, or have the butcher do this. Season with salt and pepper. Sear the tenderloin on all sides in a skillet. Let stand until cool. Roll the pastry 1/4 inch thick on a lightly floured surface. Spread the mushroom mixture down the center of the pastry and top with the tenderloin. Wrap the pastry around the tenderloin, sealing the edges with water. Arrange the pastry-wrapped tenderloin seam side down on a baking sheet. Brush with the egg yolk. Decorate with additional puff pastry using cookie cutters as desired; attach the decorations with water.

Bake for 20 to 25 minutes or until the pastry is golden brown and a meat thermometer registers 130 degrees. Slice as desired. Serves 4 to 5.

Photograph for this recipe on facing page.

Prime Rib Roast with Horseradish Sauce

1/2 cup coarsely ground pepper
1/4 cup kosher salt
1/4 cup seasoned salt

2 tablespoons granulated garlic
1 (4- to 6-pound) certified Angus
  lip-on rib roast

1 cup sour cream
1/4 to 1/3 cup prepared horseradish

This recipe requires 12 hours of refrigeration. Preheat the oven to 250 degrees. Mix the pepper, kosher salt, seasoned salt and garlic in a bowl. Sprinkle the pepper mixture over the surface of the roast; sprinkle heavier on the fat portion. Place the roast in a large shallow dish. Marinate, covered, in the refrigerator for 12 hours.

Place the roast in a deep roasting pan and tent with foil. Roast for 2 to 3 hours or until a meat thermometer registers 110 degrees. Immediately reduce the oven temperature to 180 to 200 degrees and roast until a meat thermometer registers 135 degrees for medium-rare to medium. Remove the foil from the roast and broil until brown. Let stand for 15 to 20 minutes. Slice as desired and serve with a mixture of the sour cream and horseradish.

You may use with a bone-in rib roast, decreasing the oven temperature and increasing the roasting time. For rare to medium-rare, roast to 125 to 130 degrees; for medium-well, roast to 145 to 150 degrees; and for well done roast to 155 degrees or higher. Serves 6.

Spicy Rib-Eye Roast

1/2 cup coarsely ground or
  cracked pepper
1/2 teaspoon cardamom

1 (6-pound) boneless rib-eye
  roast, trimmed
1 cup soy sauce
3/4 cup red wine vinegar

1 tablespoon tomato paste
1 teaspoon paprika
1/2 teaspoon garlic powder

This recipe requires 8 hours of refrigeration. Preheat the oven to 325 degrees. Rub a mixture of the pepper and cardamom over the surface of the roast. Place the roast in a large shallow dish. Mix the soy sauce, vinegar, tomato paste, paprika and garlic powder in a bowl and pour over the roast. Marinate, covered, in the refrigerator for 8 hours, turning occasionally; drain. Wrap the roast in foil and place in a shallow roasting pan. Insert a meat thermometer in the thickest portion of the roast, making an opening in the foil so the thermometer does not touch the foil. Bake for 2 hours or until the meat thermometer registers 145 degrees for medium-rare. Let stand before slicing. Serves 12 to 14.

Chipotle Maple Barbeque Beef Brisket

Barbeque Rub

2 tablespoons paprika

1 tablespoon black pepper

1 tablespoon kosher salt or sea salt

1 tablespoon garlic powder

1 tablespoon chili powder

1 tablespoon brown sugar

1/4 teaspoon cayenne pepper

Chipotle Maple
Barbeque Sauce

1 (28-ounce) can crushed tomatoes

1 cup white vinegar

1/2 cup maple syrup

1/2 cup apple cider or unfiltered
   apple juice

1/2 cup packed light brown sugar

3 chipotle chiles in adobo
   sauce, chopped

1/4 cup Worcestershire sauce

Juice of 2 lemons

4 garlic cloves, minced

2 tablespoons dry mustard

2 teaspoons sea salt

2 teaspoons freshly ground pepper

Beef Brisket

1 (3 1/2- to 4-pound) beef brisket,
   at room temperature

1/2 cup packed light brown sugar

1/4 cup Worcestershire sauce

2 tablespoons balsamic vinegar

1 cup beer

*T*his recipe requires 6 hours of refrigeration. Prepare a hot fire in a charcoal grill or preheat a gas grill. Preheat the oven to 350 degrees.

For the rub, combine the paprika, black pepper, salt, garlic powder, chili powder, brown sugar and cayenne pepper in a jar with a tight-fitting lid and seal tightly. Shake to mix.

For the sauce, combine the tomatoes, vinegar, syrup, apple cider, brown sugar, chipotle chiles, Worcestershire sauce and lemon juice in a heavy saucepan and mix well. Stir in the garlic, dry mustard, salt and pepper. Bring to a boil over medium-high heat. Reduce the heat and simmer for 30 to 35 minutes or until the sauce is reduced by about one-fourth and thickened, stirring occasionally.

For the brisket, score the brisket and place in a shallow dish. Sprinkle the surface of the brisket with 2 tablespoons of the rub. Mix the brown sugar, Worcestershire sauce and vinegar in a bowl and pour over the brisket, turning several times to coat. Marinate, covered, in the refrigerator for 6 to 10 hours, turning occasionally. Bring to room temperature. Drain, reserving the marinade.

Sear the brisket over hot coals for 4 to 6 minutes per side or until lightly charred. Or, sear the brisket in a skillet. Remove the brisket to a large cast-iron skillet or ovenproof skillet. Pour the reserved marinade over the brisket. Mix the beer and 1 cup of the barbeque sauce in a bowl and pour over the brisket, turning to coat.

Roast, covered with foil or a lid, for 3 1/2 hours or until the brisket shreds easily with a fork. Remove the brisket to a platter. Let stand until cool and then slice against the grain. Drizzle with the remaining barbeque sauce or serve the sauce on the side. Serves 4 to 6.

Sliced Filet with Cipolline Onions and Wild Mushrooms

4 (10-ounce) filets mignons
Kosher salt to taste

6 ounces oil-pack cipolline onions
8 ounces wild mushrooms

1/4 cup fig essence
4 ounces demi-glace

Do not prepare the mushroom mixture too far in advance or it will destroy the texture.

Preheat the grill. Season the filets heavily with salt. Grill the steaks over hot coals to the desired degree of doneness. Combine the onions and mushrooms in a hot sauté pan and cook until the mushrooms begin to soften and release moisture. Add the fig essence and toss to coat. Mound equal portions of the onion mixture in the center of four serving plates and top each serving with one filet. Drizzle 2 tablespoons of the demi-glace over each steak. Measure the fig essence carefully, as too much can cause an unwanted sweetness. One tablespoon per serving is just enough to help caramelize the vegetables. You may substitute 1/4 cup diced dried figs for the fig essence. Serves 4.

Courtesy of James Nuetzi, Executive Chef, The Capital Grille

Mongolian Beef

1 (1-pound) flank steak
3 tablespoons soy sauce
3 tablespoons vegetable oil
1 tablespoon sesame oil
1 tablespoon rice wine vinegar
1 tablespoon cornstarch

1 1/2 teaspoons sugar
3/4 teaspoon baking soda
1 tablespoon hoisin sauce
1 tablespoon hot chile sauce
1 teaspoon cornstarch
1/2 cup water

5 tablespoons vegetable oil
1 (8-ounce) can water chestnuts, drained and sliced
1 cup snow peas
8 to 10 green onions, cut into 1/2-inch lengths

This recipe requires 1 hour of refrigeration. Slice the steak diagonally across the grain into thin 3-inch strips. Mix the soy sauce, 3 tablespoons vegetable oil, the sesame oil and vinegar in a large bowl. Whisk in 1 tablespoon cornstarch, the sugar and baking soda until blended. Add the steak and turn to coat. Marinate, covered, in the refrigerator for 1 to 2 hours, turning occasionally. Mix the hoisin sauce, chile sauce, 1 teaspoon cornstarch and the water in a bowl until combined. Heat 5 tablespoons vegetable oil in a wok over high heat. Stir-fry the marinated steak strips in the hot oil for 1 minute or until light brown. Add the water chestnuts and snow peas and stir-fry for 2 minutes. Stir in the hoisin sauce mixture and bring to a boil. Add the green onions and stir-fry for 30 seconds. Serve with steamed or fried rice, soft noodles or fried rice noodles. Serves 4.

Bleu Cheese-Stuffed Tenderloin with Marinated Mushrooms

Marinated Mushrooms
1 cup (2 sticks) butter
3 onions, chopped
1¹/2 pounds fresh
    mushrooms, trimmed
1 cup dry cooking sherry
3 tablespoons lemon juice
1 teaspoon dried sweet basil
1 teaspoon crushed oregano

1 teaspoon garlic salt
1 teaspoon thyme
1 teaspoon Tabasco sauce
1 teaspoon salt

Tenderloin Steaks
2 beef tenderloin steaks
¹/4 cup (or less) crumbled
    bleu cheese

2 teaspoons half-and-half
2 tablespoons butter
3 green onions, minced
1 garlic clove, minced
¹/3 cup vermouth
2 tablespoons finely
    chopped pecans

For the mushrooms, melt the butter in a sauté pan. Sauté the onions in the butter. Add the mushrooms and stir until the mushrooms are completely coated. Stir in the sherry, lemon juice, basil, oregano, garlic salt, thyme, Tabasco sauce and salt. Simmer for 30 minutes. Remove from the heat and drain.

For the steaks, cut a pocket in the side of each steak. Mix the bleu cheese and half-and-half in a bowl and spoon the cheese mixture evenly into the pockets. Reduce the amount of bleu cheese if you do not want an obvious bleu cheese flavor.

Melt the butter in an ovenproof skillet over medium heat. Cook the green onions and garlic in the butter until the green onions are tender, stirring constantly. Remove the green onion mixture to a bowl, leaving some of the butter in the skillet. Sear the steaks in the remaining butter. Then finish in a 400-degree oven to the desired degree of doneness. Remove the steaks to a platter, reserving the pan drippings. Cover the steaks to keep warm.

Add the vermouth and pecans to the reserved pan drippings and cook for 1 to 2 minutes. Stir in the desired amount of the green onion mixture. Drizzle the sauce over the steaks. Top evenly with the mushrooms. Serve immediately. Serves 2.

Creole Mustard-Crusted Rack of Lamb

1/4 cup unseasoned dry
    bread crumbs
2 teaspoons chopped fresh
    basil leaves
1/2 teaspoon chopped
    fresh rosemary
1/2 teaspoon chopped fresh thyme

1 teaspoon Cajun seasoning
2 tablespoons olive oil
1 teaspoon Cajun seasoning
1 (4- to 6-rib) rack of lamb,
    trimmed and frenched
2 tablespoons Creole mustard or
    whole grain mustard

Preheat the oven to 450 degrees. Combine the bread crumbs, basil, rosemary, thyme and 1 teaspoon Cajun seasoning in a bowl and mix well. Add the olive oil and mix until coated. Season the lamb on both sides with 1 teaspoon Cajun seasoning. Heat a large ovenproof skillet over medium-high heat. Place the lamb fat side down in the hot skillet. Sear for 1 minute on each side including the ends, for a total of 4 minutes. Remove to a platter and cool for 10 minutes.

Spread the Creole mustard over the surface of the lamb and coat with the bread crumb mixture, patting to ensure the bread crumb mixture adheres. Place the lamb fat side up in the ovenproof skillet. Roast for 20 to 25 minutes for medium-rare. Remove from the oven and let stand for 5 minutes. Cut the rack into individual chops before serving. Serves 2.

Photograph for this recipe on page 126.

My dining room table is a long table, almost resembling a runway highlighted by a beautiful centerpiece. Most days my table remains clean and ready for family gatherings and formal events, however, it serves many other purposes, too—a drafting table for my husband, a study desk for my children, and a project center to collate and organize projects for my volunteer endeavors. Although my dining table is most grand when dressed for Thanksgiving or Christmas, the time I like best is when we are packing for a trip. When all the kids' clothes are spread out on the table, it is then that I can imagine what a great time we will have and how wonderful the photos will be with our color-coordinated outfits. At this point the trip is merely a vision, and reality has not yet set in with stained clothes, skinned knees, and moody family members.
—L. Kamasz

Leg of Lamb with Roasted Potatoes and Brown Gravy

1 (4- to 6-pound) bone-out leg of
   lamb, rolled and tied
12 to 16 garlic cloves
California blend garlic salt to taste
Freshly cracked pepper to taste

6 to 8 potatoes, sliced into sixths
Extra-virgin olive oil
1¹/₂ cups water
All-purpose flour
Sea salt to taste

Preheat the oven to 500 degrees. Rinse the lamb and pat dry. Make twelve to sixteen 1-inch-deep slits in the lamb with a pairing knife and stuff each slit with one garlic clove; use about six to eight garlic cloves per side. Coat the surface of the lamb with garlic salt and pepper. Arrange the lamb in a roasting pan. Place the roasting pan in the oven and immediately decrease the oven temperature to 350 degrees. Roast for 25 to 30 minutes per pound.

Place the potatoes in a roasting pan and coat with olive oil. Sprinkle with garlic salt and pepper. Place the potatoes in the oven 1 hour before the lamb is roasted to the desired degree of doneness. Roast the potatoes until crisp. Turn off the oven and remove the lamb, leaving the potatoes in the oven with the door closed to keep warm.

Remove the lamb to a platter, reserving the pan drippings. Let the lamb rest for 30 minutes before carving. Stir 1¹/₂ cups water into the reserved drippings and bring to a simmer over medium heat. Make a slurry with flour and a small amount of water in a bowl and gradually add to the drippings mixture, stirring constantly.

Cook the gravy to the desired consistency, stirring frequently. Season with salt and pepper. Serve the lamb and potatoes on serving plates drizzled with the gravy. Serves 6 to 8.

Fall-off-the-Bone Ribs

1 tablespoon salt
1 teaspoon smoked paprika
1 teaspoon garlic powder

1 teaspoon onion powder
1/2 teaspoon pepper
1/2 teaspoon ground cumin
2 slabs pork ribs
1 (12-ounce) can beer

1 cup water
1 1/2 cups favorite barbeque sauce
    or Chipotle Maple Barbeque
    Sauce (page 133)

Preheat the oven to 300 degrees. Preheat the grill. Mix the salt, paprika, garlic powder, onion powder, pepper and cumin in a bowl. Rinse the slabs under cold water. Make a small cut between two of the ribs on the back of one of the slabs. Place your hand under the cut (should be very superficial) and run a finger under to loosen the membrane. Pull the membrane off the entire length of the slab. Repeat this process with the remaining slab. Rinse the slabs and pat dry.

Coat the slabs with the salt mixture. Pour the beer and water into a roasting pan. Arrange the slabs on a rack in the roasting pan and cover with foil. Bake for 2 1/2 to 3 hours or until the meat begins to fall off the bone. Brush the slabs with the barbeque sauce and grill over hot coals until heated through. Or, broil until the sauce begins to bubble. Serves 4 to 6.

Photograph for this recipe on page 107.

In our home, we love all the holidays. We have formal dinners for Thanksgiving, Christmas, and Easter but mostly casual fun with friends and family such as Super Bowl, backyard barbeques, mystery dinners, birthdays, bunco, girls' night, and Valentine and Halloween potlucks. I truly love the formal dinners and events since I have so many loving memories when using my grandmother's things. I have wonderful childhood memories of family gatherings at the table with hugs, kisses, and much laughter. The excitement would make me feel all warm inside for weeks longing for the next big holiday. My husband says I go overboard for the holidays, but I want to ensure I create the same fabulous feelings and unforgettable memories for my daughter. We have traditions passed down, and one was setting the table with silver and china over an antique tablecloth. Afterwards everything was handwashed, and we would share in washing and drying each piece. I really didn't think much of it when we were small, and now I enjoy washing and drying each plate, fork, or serving piece with such care as I think of the lifelong memories we just created as a family or with friends. —E. Gogineni

Pistachio-Crusted Pork with Mustard Cream Sauce

Pork
1 1/2 cups crushed pistachios
1 cup bread crumbs
3 tablespoons olive oil
1 teaspoon salt
1 teaspoon pepper
2 pork tenderloins

1 cup grainy mustard or
   Creole mustard

Mustard Cream Sauce
1/2 cup dry white wine
1/4 cup chopped shallots
2 cups heavy whipping cream

2 tablespoons Dijon mustard or
   grainy mustard
2 tablespoons chopped fresh thyme
Salt and pepper to taste
Additional pistachios (optional)

*P*reheat the oven to 450 degrees.

For the pork, mix 1 1/2 cups pistachios, the bread crumbs, olive oil, 1 teaspoon salt and 1 teaspoon pepper in a bowl. Coat the tenderloins with the grainy mustard and then coat with the bread crumb mixture. Arrange the tenderloins on a baking sheet lined with baking parchment.

Bake for about 10 minutes or until brown. Reduce the oven temperature to 350 degrees and bake for 15 to 20 minutes or until a meat thermometer registers 155 degrees. Remove from the oven and let stand for 10 minutes before slicing.

For the sauce, bring the wine and shallots to a boil in a saucepan over high heat. Boil until the wine evaporates. Reduce the heat to medium-high and stir in the cream. Simmer until reduced to about 1 cup and the consistency of a sauce. Stir in the Dijon mustard and thyme. Season with salt and pepper to taste. Slice the pork and arrange on a serving platter. Drizzle with the mustard sauce. Garnish with additional pistachios. Serves 8.

Prosciutto Pork Tenderloin with Fennel and Apricots

1/2 cup fresh bread crumbs, lightly toasted

9 tablespoons (about) olive oil

2 tablespoons grated Parmesan cheese

2 teaspoons flat-leaf parsley, chopped

2 teaspoons fresh rosemary, chopped

2 (1- to 1 1/2-pound) pork tenderloins

8 slightly thick slices prosciutto

1 teaspoon kosher salt

1 teaspoon freshly cracked pepper

2 small fennel bulbs, cut into fourths or eights

Salt and pepper to taste

16 dried apricots

Preheat the oven to 450 degrees. Mix the bread crumbs, 3 tablespoons of the olive oil, 1 teaspoon of the parsley and 1 teaspoon of the rosemary in a bowl until the mixture adheres, adding additional oil as needed for the desired consistency.

Arrange the tenderloins on a hard surface side by side with the thick end of one tenderloin next to the thin end of the remaining tenderloin. Overlap the prosciutto slices down the length of one of the tenderloins and spread the bread crumb mixture on the prosciutto. Fold the prosciutto over to enclose the filling and place the remaining tenderloin on top of the prosciutto. Tie the tenderloins together using kitchen twine. Mix 3 tablespoons of the remaining olive oil, the remaining 1 teaspoon parsley, the remaining 1 teaspoon rosemary, 1 teaspoon salt and 1 teaspoon pepper in a bowl until the consistency of a thick paste. Rub over the surface of the tenderloins. You may prepare up to this point in advance. Wrap the tenderloins in plastic wrap and chill in the refrigerator. Bring to room temperature before proceeding with the recipe.

Place the tenderloins on a baking sheet lined with baking parchment. Toss the fennel with 2 tablespoons of the remaining olive oil in a bowl. Season with salt and pepper to taste. Arrange the fennel around the tenderloins. Bake for 15 minutes. Reduce the oven temperature to 375 degrees. Toss the apricots with the remaining 1 tablespoon olive oil in a bowl and sprinkle around the tenderloins. Bake for 20 to 30 minutes or until a meat thermometer registers 145 degrees. Let stand for 10 minutes. Remove the twine and cut into 1-inch slices. Serve with the fennel and apricots. Serves 8.

Photograph for this recipe on facing page.

Roasted Pork Tenderloin with Rosemary Fig Sauce

Pork Tenderloin

3 pounds pork tenderloin

2 tablespoons olive oil

Kosher salt and freshly ground
    pepper to taste

Rosemary Fig Sauce

2 1/2 cups tawny port

1 1/4 cups chicken broth

16 dried figs, coarsely chopped

2 sprigs of fresh rosemary

2 cinnamon sticks

1 tablespoon light brown sugar

1/4 teaspoon salt

1/8 teaspoon freshly ground pepper

1 tablespoon unsalted butter,
    cubed (optional)

Preheat the oven to 425 degrees.

For the tenderloin, line a roasting pan with baking parchment and arrange a rack in the pan. Remove any excess fat or silver skin from the tenderloin. Brush the surface with the olive oil and sprinkle with salt and pepper.

Heat a 12-inch heavy skillet over medium-high heat until a droplet of water vaporizes in 1 to 2 seconds. If the water skitters around the skillet and does not evaporate, the skillet is too hot. Remove the skillet from the heat and cool slightly. Once the pan reaches the searing temperature, place the tenderloin in the skillet.

Sear for about 2 minutes and then turn. Sear the remaining sides for about 1 minute per side or until brown on all sides. When lifting the corner of the tenderloin to turn during the searing process, it should release easily. If the tenderloin sticks, wait a few more seconds before turning so you can get an easy release. Place the tenderloin in a roasting pan. Roast for about 25 minutes or until a meat thermometer registers 170 degrees. Let stand and then slice as desired.

For the sauce, combine the wine, broth, figs, rosemary, cinnamon sticks, brown sugar, salt and pepper in a heavy saucepan. Bring to a boil over medium-high heat. Reduce the heat and cook over a gentle boil until the mixture is reduced by half.

Remove from the heat and discard the rosemary sprigs and cinnamon sticks, leaving any loose rosemary leaves in the sauce. Cool slightly and pour into a blender. Add the butter and process until smooth and creamy. If the sauce is thin, continue to process until creamy. Serve with the pork. Serves 10 to 12.

Easter Pork Loin with Vegetables and Orange Sage Sauce

1 (3-pound) boneless pork loin roast, trimmed and tied
1/2 teaspoon kosher salt
1/4 teaspoon ground pepper
1 tablespoon unsalted butter
2 1/2 pounds small red potatoes, peeled around the diameter
1 pound baby carrots

1 to 2 tablespoons extra-virgin olive oil
1/2 teaspoon kosher salt
1/4 teaspoon ground pepper
1/4 cup dry white wine
1 yellow onion, chopped
1 (10-ounce) can reduced-sodium chicken broth

1 tablespoon Dijon mustard
2 teaspoons snipped fresh sage
1/3 cup fresh orange juice
1 tablespoon cornstarch
Sprigs of fresh sage (optional)
Orange slices (optional)

Preheat the oven to 375 degrees. Sprinkle the pork with 1/2 teaspoon salt and 1/4 teaspoon pepper. Melt the butter in a skillet over medium-high heat. Sear the pork in the butter for 1 minute on each side or until brown. Remove the pork to a large roasting pan, reserving the pan dripping.

Toss the potatoes, carrots, olive oil, 1/2 teaspoon salt and 1/4 teaspoon pepper in a bowl until the vegetables are coated. Scatter the potato mixture around the pork. Bake for 55 to 65 minutes or until a meat thermometer registers 160 degrees. Let the pork stand for 15 minutes before slicing.

Heat the reserved pan drippings in the skillet over medium-high heat. Deglaze the skillet with the wine. Add the onion and cook for 4 minutes or until the onion is tender. Stir in the broth, Dijon mustard and snipped sage and bring to a boil. Reduce the heat to low and simmer for 3 minutes.

Mix the orange juice and cornstarch in a small bowl until blended. Add to the broth mixture and bring to a boil. Cook until thickened and of a sauce consistency, stirring frequently. Slice the pork and arrange on a serving platter encircled with the potatoes and carrots. Drizzle with the orange sauce. Garnish with sprigs of sage and orange slices. Serves 8.

Smothered Seared Pork Chops

4 (1-inch-thick) bone-in
   pork chops
2 tablespoons olive oil
1/4 teaspoon salt
1 teaspoon pepper

1 tablespoon olive oil
2 yellow onions, thinly sliced
1 tablespoon all-purpose flour
2 red bell peppers, roasted, peeled,
   seeded and cut into strips
1/4 cup white wine (not too sweet)

2 tablespoons apple cider vinegar
2 tablespoons capers
1 cup chicken broth
1 tablespoon chopped
   flat-leaf parsley
Salt and pepper to taste

Preheat the oven to 375 degrees. Coat the chops with 2 tablespoons olive oil and season with 1/4 teaspoon salt and 1 teaspoon pepper. Sear the chops on both sides in a hot cast-iron skillet. Remove the chops to a baking sheet, reserving the pan drippings. Bake for about 10 minutes or until a meat thermometer registers 145 degrees.

Heat 1 tablespoon olive oil with the reserved pan drippings. Add the onions and sauté for 15 minutes or until the onions are tender. Mix in the flour and sauté for 2 minutes. Stir in the bell peppers, wine, vinegar and capers. Cook for 1 minute. Add the broth and bring to a boil. Cook the sauce until the desired consistency. Stir in the parsley and season with salt and pepper to taste. Drizzle over the chops. Serves 4.

Our dining room is furnished with a tiger oak table and a beautiful buffet to match. The table is special because my husband's father bought it from an antique store when he was a child. We've had it refinished, and the guy who did the work for us said that the piece of furniture is over one hundred years old. So, the memories are there—even before we were.

We use our dining table for everything, from game night with friends and family to dinner parties, business meetings, and bible studies. I even use it to wrap all of our Christmas presents each year. At those times it stays messy, but it doesn't bother me because I love gift giving!

One Thanksgiving, my parents and several family members stayed at our home while we went to the beach (they were there for treatments at MD Anderson). Before I left, I set the table with a beautiful setting—one that I knew they would enjoy. When we came home, the aunties said they felt so pleased and pampered eating at a beautiful table that was set with them in mind.   —B. Buck

Veal Piccata with Angel Hair Pasta

8 ounces angel hair pasta

Salt to taste

2 tablespoons extra-virgin olive oil

3 tablespoons plus 1 teaspoon chopped fresh parsley

2 tablespoons freshly grated Parmigiano-Reggiano cheese

2 1/2 teaspoons salt

1 3/4 teaspoons freshly ground pepper

2 teaspoons chopped fresh basil

1 cup all-purpose flour

8 (2 1/2- to 3-ounce) veal medallions, pounded 1/4-inch thick

2 tablespoons olive oil

1 tablespoon unsalted butter

1/2 cup dry white wine

1/4 cup low-sodium chicken broth

2 tablespoons fresh lemon juice

2 tablespoon capers, drained

2 teaspoons minced garlic

2 tablespoons unsalted butter

*B*ring a large saucepan of salted water to a boil. Add the pasta and cook for 4 minutes or until al dente, stirring frequently to separate the strands. Drain in a colander and return to the saucepan. Add 2 tablespoons olive oil, 2 tablespoons of the parsley, the cheese, 1/2 teaspoon of the salt, 1/4 teaspoon of the pepper and the basil and toss to coat. Cover to keep warm.

Mix the flour with 1 teaspoon salt and 1 teaspoon pepper in a shallow dish. Season the medallions with the remaining 1 teaspoon salt and the remaining 1/2 teaspoon pepper. Coat the medallions one at a time with the flour mixture, shaking to remove any excess.

Heat 2 tablespoons olive oil and 1 tablespoon butter in a large skillet or sauté pan over medium-high heat until the butter melts. Cook the medallions in batches in the olive oil mixture for 1 to 1 1/2 minutes per side or until light golden brown and just cooked through. Remove the medallions to paper towels to drain, reserving the pan drippings.

Add the wine to the reserved pan drippings and bring to a boil, stirring with a wooden spoon to loosen any brown bits. Cook for 2 to 3 minutes or until the wine is reduced by half, stirring frequently. Add the broth, lemon juice, capers and garlic and bring to a boil. Cook for 4 minutes or until thickened and of a sauce consistency. Stir in 2 tablespoons butter and 1 tablespoon of the remaining parsley. Cook until the butter melts. Return the medallions to the skillet and cook for about 1 minute or until heated through.

Mound the pasta evenly on four large serving plates. Arrange two medallions on each serving. Spoon the sauce over the veal and garnish each serving with the remaining 1 teaspoon parsley. Serve immediately. Serves 4.

Did You Know?

A European place setting has the fork tines and soup spoon placed down rather than facing up.

Boursin-Stuffed Veal Chops

4 ounces pancetta
8 ounces cream cheese, softened
10 ounces boursin cheese with
    fines herbes and pepper
1/4 teaspoon salt
1/4 teaspoon pepper

1/4 bunch green onions, chopped
4 bone-in veal chops, frenched
2 tablespoons olive oil
2 garlic cloves, minced
2 tablespoons chopped
    flat-leaf parsley

2 teaspoons kosher salt
1 teaspoon pepper
Olive oil for searing
1 cup (about) red wine
1 1/4 to 1 1/2 cups beef stock
1 tablespoon cornstarch

This recipe requires 2 hours of refrigeration. Preheat the oven to 375 degrees.

Bake the pancetta in a baking pan for 10 minutes or until brown and crisp; drain. Let stand until cool and then crumble. Process the pancetta, cream cheese, boursin cheese, 1/4 teaspoon salt and 1/4 teaspoon pepper in a food processor until combined. Stir in the green onions. Spoon the boursin mixture into a pastry bag.

Make a small hole in one of the veal chops directly above the bone using a boning knife. Stick the tip of the knife in the hole and rotate the knife 180 degrees to form a small pocket. Stick the tip of the pastry bag as far inside the chop as possible and fill with the boursin mixture. Repeat the process with the remaining chops and remaining boursin mixture.

Mix 2 tablespoons olive oil, the garlic, parsley, 2 teaspoons salt and 1 teaspoon pepper in a shallow dish. Add the chops and turn to coat. Marinate, covered, in the refrigerator for 2 to 12 hours. Bring to room temperature before proceeding with the recipe.

Sear the chops on both sides in olive oil in a skillet for about 3 minutes. Remove the chops to a baking pan lined with baking parchment, reserving the pan drippings. Bake the chops for 15 to 25 minutes or until firm to the touch and the juices run clear.

Deglaze the skillet with the wine, stirring with a wooden spoon to dislodge any browned bits. Stir in the stock and simmer until the mixture is reduced by half. Mix the cornstarch with several ounces of water in a bowl until smooth and add to the wine sauce. Cook until thickened and of a sauce consistency, stirring constantly. Adjust the seasonings as desired.

Drizzle with the wine sauce. Great served with Israeli Couscous on page 125. Serves 4.

Photograph for this recipe on facing page.

Osso Buco

4 (16-ounce) veal shanks
Salt and pepper to taste
1/2 cup all-purpose flour
3 tablespoons olive oil
3 carrots, finely chopped

8 ribs celery, finely chopped
2 onions, finely chopped
2 tomatoes, peeled, seeded
 and chopped
1 tablespoon lemon zest

1/2 cup white wine
1 1/2 cups veal stock or chicken
 stock
6 sprigs thyme
2 bay leaves

Preheat the oven to 300 degrees. Season the shanks with salt and pepper. Coat with the flour, shaking off any excess. Heat a large ovenproof roasting pan until hot. Pour the olive oil into the pan and heat until the oil smokes. Sear the shanks in the hot oil until brown on all sides. Remove the shanks to a platter, reserving the pan drippings.

Add the carrots, celery, onions, tomatoes and lemon zest to the reserved pan drippings and cook until the vegetables wilt. Return the shanks to the pan and add the wine, stock, thyme and bay leaves. Bake, covered, for 1 1/2 to 2 hours or until the meat falls off the bones. Discard the thyme sprigs and bay leaves. Remove the shanks to a heated platter and pour the vegetable sauce over the shanks. If the sauce is too thin, cook over high heat to the desired consistency. Serves 4.

Chicken Rollatini

4 boneless skinless chicken breasts
8 ounces pancetta, thinly sliced
1 cup baby spinach, chopped

4 ounces goat cheese, crumbled
2 tablespoons Dijon Country
 mustard

1 cup seasoned bread crumbs
2 tablespoons olive oil

Preheat the oven to 400 degrees. Pound the chicken 1/4 inch thick between sheets of heavy-duty plastic wrap. Top the chicken breasts with equal portions of the pancetta. Mix the spinach and cheese in a bowl and spread over the pancetta. Roll to enclose the filling and secure with wooden picks. Brush the Dijon mustard over the surface of the chicken rolls and coat with the bread crumbs.

Heat the olive oil in a large ovenproof sauté pan over medium to high heat. Cook the chicken rolls in the hot oil until brown on all sides. Bake for 18 to 22 minutes or until the chicken is cooked through. Serves 4.

Chicken Breasts Lombardy

2 tablespoons butter
8 ounces fresh mushrooms, sliced
6 boneless skinless chicken breasts
1/2 cup all-purpose flour
1/3 cup butter

3/4 cup marsala wine
1/2 cup chicken broth
1/2 teaspoon salt
1/8 teaspoon pepper
1/2 cup (2 ounces) shredded
   mozzarella cheese

1/2 cup (2 ounces) grated
   Parmesan cheese
2 green onions, chopped

Preheat the oven to 450 degrees. Melt 2 tablespoons butter in a large nonstick skillet over medium heat and add the mushrooms. Cook for 3 to 5 minutes or just until the mushrooms are tender, stirring constantly. Remove from the heat.

Cut each chicken breast lengthwise into halves. Pound the chicken 1/8 inch thick between sheets of heavy-duty plastic wrap using a rolling pin or the flat side of a meat mallet. Coat the chicken with the flour. Cook the chicken in batches in 1 to 2 tablespoons of the 1/3 cup butter at a time in a large nonstick skillet over medium heat for 3 to 4 minutes per side or until golden brown. Arrange the chicken with edges overlapping in a lightly greased 9×13-inch baking dish, reserving the pan drippings. Sprinkle the mushrooms over the chicken.

Add the wine and broth to the reserved pan drippings and bring to a boil. Reduce the heat and simmer for 10 minutes, stirring occasionally. Stir in the salt and pepper and pour over the chicken. Mix the mozzarella cheese, Parmesan cheese and green onions in a bowl and sprinkle over the top. Bake for 12 to 14 minutes or until the cheese melts and the chicken is cooked through. You may substitute a mixture of 2/3 cup dry wine and 2 tablespoons brandy for the marsala. Serves 6.

At our house the biggest holiday is Thanksgiving. We go all out with the china, crystal, and silver; we have candles and a fall centerpiece of gourds and flowers. I start planning and stocking food the week before. I usually start cooking on Monday, and anything that can be made in advance is cooked and just warmed up that day. By doing this, I am able to relax on Thanksgiving Day and enjoy time with family. That was not the case in 1987. Now, I had planned the whole meal and had cooked almost all of it and set the food aside in the fridge when I went into labor with my daughter. My husband had his dinner in the hospital cafeteria between contractions, and I didn't even get turkey that day! My daughter was born at 2:14 p.m., and we called her our little turkey baby. We finally had our Thanksgiving feast the day we came home. We had a little extra to be thankful for that year!   —J. Jewell

Whole Roasted Chicken with Jalapeño Butter

Roasted Chicken

1/4 cup Dijon mustard or grainy
    mustard
3 tablespoons olive oil
1 1/2 teaspoons water
1 1/2 teaspoons ancho chile powder
3 1/2 garlic cloves, minced
1/2 teaspoon salt
1/2 teaspoon freshly ground pepper
1 (4-pound) chicken
1/4 cup brine (Juice drained from
    pickled jalapeño peppers)

Jalapeño Crumb Topping

2 tablespoons pickled jalapeño
    peppers, sliced
2 tablespoons fresh orange juice
3 1/2 garlic cloves, minced
2 tablespoons unsalted butter
1 cup bread crumbs or panko
1 tablespoon chopped cilantro
Zest of 1 lemon
1/4 teaspoon cayenne pepper
Salt and freshly ground black
    pepper to taste

Preheat the oven to 350 degrees.

For the chicken, process the Dijon mustard, olive oil, water, ancho chile powder, garlic, salt and pepper in a blender until puréed. Place the chicken, breast side up, on a baking sheet with sides. Coat with the mustard purée.

Bake for 70 minutes or until the chicken is cooked through, covering with foil after 30 minutes to prevent overbrowning. Brush the chicken with half the brine and bake for 5 minutes longer. Remove the chicken from the oven and coat with the remaining brine. Let stand for 10 minutes

For the topping, sauté the jalapeño peppers, orange juice and garlic in the butter in a sauté pan. Add the bread crumbs, cilantro, lemon zest and cayenne pepper and cook until the bread crumbs are light brown. Season with salt and black pepper. Sprinkle over the chicken and serve. Serves 4.

Photograph for this recipe on facing page.

Chicken Breasts Stuffed with Spinach and Sun-Dried Tomatoes

1 tablespoon olive oil
2 garlic cloves, minced
10 ounces fresh spinach, blanched
and drained
6 sun-dried tomatoes (oil-packed),
drained and chopped

1/2 teaspoon salt
1/2 teaspoon pepper
1/4 teaspoon dried thyme
1/4 cup goat cheese
1/3 cup cream cheese, softened
6 to 8 boneless skinless
chicken breasts

Salt and pepper to taste
1 1/2 cups chicken stock
Zest of 1/2 lemon
2 teaspoons fresh lemon juice
2 teaspoons Dijon mustard
1 tablespoon olive oil
Juice of 1/2 lemon (optional)

Using baby spinach for this dish saves time and effort. Not only is baby spinach cleaner, but the stems and leaves are tender and do not need to be chopped for final preparation. If using large spinach leaves, be sure to rinse well, remove the tough stems, and chop the leaves before cooking and adding to the rest of the ingredients.

Heat 1 tablespoons olive oil in a sauté pan over medium heat. Cook the garlic in the hot oil for 1 minute. Stir in the spinach, sun-dried tomatoes, 1/2 teaspoon salt, 1/2 teaspoon pepper and the thyme. Cook for 2 minutes. Spoon the spinach mixture into a bowl and mix in the goat cheese and cream cheese.

Pound the chicken breasts between sheets of heavy-duty plastic wrap on a hard surface. Spread equal portions of the spinach mixture on each chicken breast. Roll to enclose the filling. Season with salt and pepper to taste.

Mix the stock, lemon zest, 2 teaspoons lemon juice and the Dijon mustard in a bowl. Heat 1 tablespoon olive oil in a large sauté pan over medium-high heat and add the chicken. Cook for 4 minutes per side or until golden brown and cooked through. Remove the chicken to a platter, reserving the pan drippings. Add the stock mixture to the reserved pan drippings and stir to loosen any brown bits from the bottom of the pan.

Cook for about 8 minutes or until the stock is reduced by half, making a light sauce. Pour over the chicken and serve. Drizzle with the juice of 1/2 lemon. You may substitute 10 ounces drained thawed frozen spinach for the fresh spinach. Serves 4.

Pan-Seared Chicken Breasts with Red Bell Pepper and Caper Sauce

Red Bell Pepper and Caper Sauce

2 tablespoons olive oil
1 large red bell pepper, chopped
3/4 cup chopped yellow onion
6 garlic cloves, minced
1 1/2 teaspoons dried basil
3/4 cup dry white wine
1 (28-ounce) can diced tomatoes
3 tablespoons capers
1 teaspoon salt
1/2 teaspoon black pepper
1/4 teaspoon red pepper flakes

Pan-Seared Chicken

4 to 6 boneless skinless
    chicken breasts
1 teaspoon salt
1/2 teaspoon black pepper
1/2 cup all-purpose flour
1 1/2 tablespoons olive oil
1 1/2 tablespoons butter
1/4 cup fresh basil, chopped
Shaved or shredded Parmesan
    cheese to taste

For the sauce, heat the olive oil in a heavy sauté pan. Add the bell pepper, onion, garlic and basil and sauté for about 5 minutes or until the onion is tender. Stir in the wine and simmer until reduced by half. Add the undrained tomatoes, capers, salt, black pepper and red pepper flakes and mix well. Bring to a boil; reduce the heat to low. Cook for about 20 minutes or until thickened, stirring occasionally. Remove from the heat and cover to keep warm.

For the chicken, sprinkle both sides of the chicken with the salt and black pepper. Coat with the flour, shaking off any excess. Heat the olive oil and butter in a 9-inch skillet over high heat until the butter melts. Add the chicken and cook for 4 minutes. Decrease the heat to medium-high and turn the chicken. Cook for 4 to 6 minutes or until cooked through. Keep warm in a 200-degree oven if the sauce is not ready. Arrange one chicken breast on each of four to six serving plates. Drizzle generously with the sauce and sprinkle with the basil and cheese. Serves 4 to 6.

Roasted Chicken with Goat Cheese-Macadamia Nut Crust

1 cup couscous
1/4 cup pimentos, drained
2 tablespoons chopped
    flat-leaf parsley
1/4 cup pine nuts, toasted

Juice of 1/2 to 1 lemon, or to taste
Salt and pepper to taste
4 (6-ounce) boneless skinless
    chicken breasts
1/4 cup honey mustard
1 teaspoon salt

1/2 teaspoon cracked pepper
8 ounces goat cheese,
    at room temperature
2 cups macadamia nuts, toasted,
    salted and chopped

Preheat the oven to 400 degrees. Prepare the couscous using the package directions. Fluff the couscous with a fork and stir in the pimentos, parsley, pine nuts and lemon juice. Season with salt and pepper to taste. Let stand until room temperature.

Coat the chicken with the honey mustard and sprinkle with 1 teaspoon salt and 1/2 teaspoon pepper. Spread a thin layer of the cheese over one side of the chicken breasts and press the macadamia nuts into the cheese. Arrange in a baking pan lined with baking parchment or sprayed with nonstick cooking spray. Bake, covered with foil, for about 20 minutes; remove the foil. Bake for 5 minutes longer or until the chicken is cooked through. Serve the chicken over the couscous on serving plates. Serves 4.

Royal Chicken

4 boneless skinless chicken breasts
Salt and pepper to taste
Fresh spinach leaves to taste

1 (5-ounce) package herbed
    boursin cheese, cut into quarters
1/2 cup walnuts, finely chopped

1/2 cup seasoned bread crumbs
3 tablespoons butter, melted

Preheat the oven to 350 degrees. Pound the chicken breasts 1/4 inch thick between sheets of heavy-duty plastic wrap. Sprinkle the chicken with salt and pepper and layer each with a few spinach leaves. Roll the cheese quarters in the walnuts until coated and top each chicken breast with one cheese quarter. Roll the chicken around the cheese until enclosed and secure with wooden picks. Lightly dust with the bread crumbs and season with salt and pepper. Arrange the chicken in a baking pan. Bake, covered, for 20 to 30 minutes or until the chicken is fork-tender, basting with the butter twice. Remove from the oven and cool for 5 minutes. Slice each roll diagonally into 1-inch-thick rounds. Serves 4.

Sticky Chicken

3 to 5 tablespoons vegetable oil
12 skinless chicken legs or boneless
    skinless thighs
1 teaspoon red pepper
Salt to taste

2 cups all-purpose flour
2 cups finely chopped onions
1 tablespoon minced garlic
2 or 3 green bell peppers, chopped
2 cups water

1 to 2 teaspoons pickled jalapeño
    pepper juice (optional)
4 to 6 cups hot cooked white rice

Heat the oil in a large Dutch oven. Season the chicken with the red pepper and salt. Pour the flour into a sealable plastic bag. Add the chicken in batches to the flour and shake to coat.

Fry the chicken in the hot oil, adding the onions, garlic, bell peppers and water after the chicken begins to brown. The onions will break down and the flour will mix with the water to form a roux. Stir in the jalapeño pepper juice for a spicier flavor. Simmer for 1 hour or longer or until the chicken is cooked through and sticky. Serve over the hot cooked rice. Add 1 tablespoon Kitchen Bouquet to darken the roux, or for a thicker roux add a sprinkle of dry roux powder. Serves 6 to 10.

Champagne Chicken

4 chicken breasts
1 teaspoon thyme
1 teaspoon seasoned salt
Dash of garlic powder
6 tablespoon butter

2/3 cup Champagne
2 teaspoons all-purpose flour
1 cup whipping cream
Hot cooked noodles or rice
Salt and pepper to taste

Sprinkle the chicken with the thyme, seasoned salt and garlic powder. Brown the chicken on both sides in the butter in a skillet. Pour the Champagne into the skillet.

Simmer, covered, for 30 to 40 minutes or until the chicken is cooked through. Remove the chicken to a platter, reserving the pan juices. Add the flour to the reserved pan juices and mix well. Stir in the cream. Season with salt and pepper.

Cook until thickened and of a sauce consistency, stirring frequently. Mound hot cooked noodles on four serving plates. Top each serving with one chicken breast and drizzle with the sauce. Serves 4.

Making a Roux

A roux is a mixture of melted butter or vegetable oil and all-purpose flour that is cooked over medium-low heat and then used to thicken mixtures. Liquid is gradually whisked into the roux and the mixture is cooked for two to three minutes, until thickened, or just long enough to cook off the flour taste but not to color. Roux is the foundation for many classic French sauces and is also used to thicken soups and some dessert sauces. Roux used in Cajun and Creole gumbos can be cooked from golden to dark brown in color to add depth and flavor.

Spicy Fried Chicken

1 1/2 cups all-purpose flour
1 teaspoon salt
1 teaspoon cayenne pepper
1 teaspoon black pepper
1 teaspoon garlic powder

2 cups hot pepper sauce
2 eggs
1 (2 1/2-pound) chicken, cut up
Vegetable oil or peanut oil

*T*his recipe requires 55 minutes of refrigeration. Combine the flour, salt, cayenne pepper, black pepper and garlic powder in a sealable plastic bag and seal tightly. Shake to mix. Whisk the hot sauce and eggs in a bowl until combined. Add the chicken and turn to coat.

Marinate in the refrigerator for 15 minutes. Turn the chicken and marinate for 10 minutes longer. The chicken may be marinated for up to 6 hours. The longer marinating time does not yield spicier chicken. Remove one piece of the chicken at a time, draining any excess marinade. Add the chicken to the seasoned flour and seal the bag tightly. Shake to coat. You may coat two pieces at a time.

Arrange the chicken on a baking sheet. Repeat this process until all of the chicken pieces are coated with the seasoned flour. Chill for 30 minutes or longer. Coat the chicken pieces again in batches in the seasoned flour.

Pour enough oil into a deep skillet to fill no more than half full and heat to 350 degrees over medium heat. Deep-fry the chicken in the hot oil for 8 to 10 minutes for white meat and 13 to 14 minutes for dark meat or until cooked through and brown and crisp on all sides. Drain on a baking sheet lined with paper towels. Serve immediately. Serves 4.

Photograph for this recipe on facing page.

Deep Frying

Establishing a system in your kitchen before you begin to deep-fry will make the process more efficient and less messy. Arrange dishes beforehand so that food can be moved directly from the marinade to the dry ingredients and then to the oil. Place a baking sheet lined with paper towels beside the skillet to drain the chicken straight from the skillet. Coat only the amount of chicken that you plan on eating immediately. Coating food too far in advance may cause the coating to become dense and gummy.

Enchiladas Suizas

1/2 cup chopped onion
1 garlic clove, minced
1 tablespoon vegetable oil
2 cups chopped cooked chicken
1 (7-ounce) can green chile salsa
1/4 cup canned chopped
   green chiles

2 tablespoons chopped cilantro
2 teaspoons all-purpose flour
1/2 teaspoon salt
1 chicken bouillon cube
Dash of paprika
1 cup milk
1/2 cup whipping cream

1/2 cup (2 ounces) shredded
   Monterey Jack cheese
1/4 cup (or more) vegetable oil
6 corn or flour tortillas
1 cup (4 ounces) shredded
   Monterey Jack cheese
Additional green chile salsa
   (optional)

Preheat the oven to 350 degrees. Sauté the onion and garlic in 1 tablespoon oil in a skillet until the onion is tender. Combine the onion mixture, chicken, 7 ounces green chile salsa, the green chiles and cilantro in a bowl and mix well. Mix the flour, salt, bouillon cube and paprika in a small saucepan. Stir in the milk and bring to a boil. Boil until slightly thickened. Remove from the heat and stir in the cream and 1/2 cup of the cheese until blended.

Heat 1/4 cup oil in a medium skillet. Soften the tortillas one at a time in the hot oil, adding additional oil as needed. Dip the tortillas in the cheese sauce and spoon a generous 1/3 cup of the chicken mixture down the center of each tortilla. Roll to enclose the filling and arrange seam side down in an 8×12-inch baking dish. Pour the remaining cheese sauce over the top and sprinkle with the remaining 1 cup cheese. Bake, covered with foil, for 15 minutes. Remove the foil and bake for 15 minutes or until heated through. Spoon additional green chile salsa down the center and serve immediately. You may soften the tortillas in chicken broth for a lighter version. Serves 6.

Photograph for this recipe on page 173.

Our kitchen table has always been a hub for our family. I've often thought, "If only the wood could speak, oh, the stories it could tell." Our kitchen table once belonged to my mother-in-law and served as her dining room table. I always admired its lovely mahogany wood and beautiful claw feet. When she was breaking up her home, I asked if I could have the table, and she was thrilled. It has held a place of honor in our kitchen ever since. The table is large; hence we often use it when guests are with us, as the kitchen area just seems to have a flowing informality, which we love. I love this table and the life it brings to our family. —L. Martens

Red Snapper with Champagne Sauce

Red Snapper
4 (8-ounce) red snapper fillets
2 tablespoons olive oil
1 tablespoon minced garlic
Salt and pepper to taste
1/4 cup olive oil

**Champagne Sauce
and Assembly**
1/2 cup Champagne
1 shallot, finely chopped
2 tablespoons minced garlic
1 1/2 to 2 tablespoons fresh
   lemon juice

1/4 cup heavy cream
3/4 cup (1 1/2 sticks) butter,
   chopped
Salt and pepper to taste
1 cup jumbo lump crab meat,
   shells removed
1/2 bunch spinach, sautéed, or
   sautéed broccolini (optional)
4 bunches Champagne grapes
   (optional)
4 crab claws (optional)
Chives (optional)

For the snapper, rub the snapper with 2 tablespoons olive oil, the garlic, salt and pepper. Sear the snapper in 1/4 cup olive oil in a sauté pan over high heat for 3 minutes per side.

For the sauce, combine the Champagne, shallot and garlic in a saucepan. Cook until the Champagne is reduced by two-thirds. Stir in the lemon juice and simmer. Whisk in the cream and stir in the butter. Season with salt and pepper. Mix in the crab meat and simmer just until heated through.

Arrange one snapper fillet on each of four serving plates. Spoon equal portions of the sauce over each. Garnish with the spinach, grapes, crab claws and chives. Serve immediately. Serves 4.

Snapper Amerigo's

1 (12-ounce) red snapper fillet	2 tablespoons unsalted butter
Salt and pepper to taste	1 garlic clove, minced
1/2 cup all-purpose flour	Juice of 1 lemon
1 to 2 tablespoons olive oil	8 ounces spinach
1 ounce Roma tomatoes, chopped	2 ounces jumbo crab meat
1/2 cup white wine	1/2 ounce green onions

Season the snapper fillet with salt and pepper and dust with the flour. Sauté in half the olive oil in a skillet for 30 seconds per side. Add the tomatoes, wine, butter, half the garlic and the lemon juice and sauté for 10 seconds.

Combine the remaining olive oil, remaining garlic and spinach in a hot skillet and sauté for 10 seconds. Season with salt and pepper. Mound the spinach on a serving plate and place the snapper fillet over the spinach. Top with the crab meat and green onions. Season with salt and pepper. Serves 1.

Courtest of Amerigo's Grille, Executive Chef Arturo Osorio

Apricot Sea Bass

1/2 cup apricot preserves	Salt and black pepper to taste
1/4 cup orange juice	4 sea bass fillets
2 tablespoons lime juice	2 tablespoons olive oil
2 teaspoons crushed garlic	Wilted spinach
1 teaspoon red pepper flakes	

Mix the preserves, orange juice, lime juice, garlic, red pepper flakes, salt and black pepper in a small saucepan. Cook for about 5 minutes or to the desired consistency. Remove from the heat and cover to keep warm.

Sauté the sea bass in the olive oil in a nonstick skillet over medium heat for 5 minutes per side or until golden brown, turning once. Arrange the sea bass over wilted spinach on serving plates and spoon the apricot sauce over the top. Serves 4.

Photograph for this recipe on facing page.

Parmesan-Crusted Turkey Cutlets

1¹/3 pounds turkey cutlets
2 eggs
1 tablespoon water
¹/4 teaspoon salt
¹/4 teaspoon pepper
1 cup (4 ounces) grated
   Parmigiano-Reggiano cheese

2 tablespoon finely chopped
   flat-leaf parsley
¹/2 cup flour
2 tablespoons unsalted butter
2 tablespoons olive oil

Pound the turkey cutlets between sheets of plastic wrap with a meat mallet or heavy plate until ¹/2 inch thick.

Combine the eggs, water, salt, pepper, cheese and parsley in a shallow bowl. Place the flour in a shallow bowl. Heat 1 tablespoon of the butter and 1 tablespoon of the olive oil in a nonstick skillet over medium-high heat until the foam subsides. Dredge half the cutlets one at a time in the flour and then in the batter, allowing any excess batter to drip off before adding to the skillet. Do not crowd the skillet. Cook for about 4 minutes or until golden brown, turning once. Remove to a heated platter. Repeat with the remaining butter, olive oil and cutlets. Serves 4.

Seared Tuna with Wasabi Mash

Lime Dressing

1/2 cup olive oil
3 tablespoons chopped
   Italian parsley
3 tablespoons chopped cilantro
2 shallots, coarsely chopped
2 garlic cloves, minced
1 tablespoon rice vinegar
Juice of 2 limes
Salt and pepper to taste

Wasabi Mash

3 pounds white potatoes or Yukon
   Gold potatoes, peeled and
   coarsely chopped
1 to 1 1/2 tablespoons
   wasabi powder
1 tablespoon water
3/4 cup milk
1/4 cup (1/2 stick) butter
Salt and pepper to taste

Seared Tuna and Assembly

6 (3/4-inch-thick) tuna fillets
Salt and pepper to taste
2 tablespoons olive oil
1 tablespoon black sesame seeds
   (optional)
2 cups radish sprouts (optional)

For the dressing, whisk the olive oil, parsley, cilantro, shallots, garlic, vinegar and lime juice in a bowl until combined. Season with salt and pepper.

For the mash, combine the potatoes with enough water to cover in a saucepan. Bring to a boil and boil for about 25 minutes or until tender. Mix the wasabi powder and 1 tablespoon water in a bowl. Let stand for 5 minutes; stir in the milk. Drain the potatoes. Add the butter and mash lightly. Stir in the milk mixture and mash lightly. Season with salt and pepper. Cover to keep warm.

For the tuna, season the tuna with salt and pepper. Heat the olive oil in a skillet over high heat just until the oil begins to smoke. Sear the tuna in the hot oil for 3 minutes per side or until brown. Remove from the heat and cool for 5 minutes.

Cut the tuna into 1/4-inch slices. Mound equal portions of the wasabi mash on six serving plates. Top each portion with the tuna and drizzle with the dressing. Garnish the tuna with sesame seeds and sprouts. Serves 6.

Crab Meat au Gratin

1 bunch green onions, chopped
1 large sweet onion, chopped
2 or 3 ribs celery, chopped
1 to 2 teaspoons minced garlic
1 cup (2 sticks) butter
3 to 4 tablespoons all-purpose flour

2 cups half-and-half
2 egg yolks, beaten
2 pounds lump white crab meat,
    drained and shells removed
3/4 cup (3 ounces) shredded
    Cheddar cheese

Salt and black pepper to taste
Red pepper or Cajun seasoning
    blend to taste
3/4 cup (3 ounces) shredded
    Cheddar cheese

Preheat the oven to 375 degrees. Reserve a few green onions for topping. Sauté the remaining green onions, sweet onion, celery and garlic in the butter in a skillet until the onions and celery are tender. Mix in the flour. Add the half-and-half and mix well. Simmer for 3 minutes or until slightly thickened. Remove from the heat and stir some of the hot mixture into the egg yolks. Stir the egg yolks into the hot mixture. Stir in the crab meat and 3/4 cup cheese. Season with salt, black pepper and red pepper. Spoon the crab meat mixture into individual ramekins or a baking dish. Sprinkle with the reserved green onions and 3/4 cup cheese. Bake for about 30 minutes. Serve with a salad and garlic bread. You may substitute claw crab meat for the lump crab meat. This can also be served as an appetizer or as a topping for grilled or sautéed fish. Serves 6.

Crawfish and Corn Maque Choux

1/4 cup (1/2 stick) butter
3 cups fresh corn kernels
1 (10-ounce) can tomatoes with
    green chiles, drained
1/2 cup chicken stock
1 cup chopped onion

1/2 cup chopped bell pepper
1/2 cup chopped celery
2 cups heavy cream
2 teaspoons minced garlic
2 teaspoons Creole seasoning
1 teaspoon salt
1 teaspoon hot pepper sauce

1 pound peeled Louisiana
    crawfish tails
3 tablespoons chopped scallions
2 tablespoons minced flat-leaf
    parsley
Hot cooked rice

Melt the butter in a medium saucepan over medium heat. Add the corn and sauté for 2 minutes. Add the tomatoes with green chiles, stock, onion, bell pepper and celery. Increase the heat and cook until the stock evaporates. Stir in the cream, garlic, Creole seasoning, salt and hot sauce and bring to a boil. Stir in the crawfish tails. Reduce the heat and simmer for 10 to 12 minutes or until the mixture begins to reduce and thicken. Stir in the scallions and parsley. Serve over or with hot cooked rice. Decrease the amount of cream if you prefer a less creamy texture. Serves 6.

Crawfish Étouffée—The Texas Way

1/2 cup (1 stick) butter
2 cups chopped onions
1 cup chopped celery
1 cup chopped bell pepper
1 garlic clove, minced
1 pound peeled crawfish tails

2 bay leaves
1 tablespoon all-purpose flour
1 cup cold water
1 1/2 teaspoons Creole seasoning
1/4 teaspoon cayenne pepper

1 (10-ounce) can cream of golden
    mushroom soup
3 tablespoons chopped green onions
2 tablespoons chopped parsley
Hot cooked rice

Melt the butter in a large skillet over medium-high heat. Add the onions, celery, bell pepper and garlic and mix well. Sauté for 10 to 12 minutes or until the vegetables are tender and golden brown. Stir in the crawfish and bay leaves. Reduce the heat to medium. Cook for 10 to 12 minutes, stirring occasionally. Dissolve the flour in the cold water in a small bowl and add to the crawfish mixture. Stir in the Creole seasoning and cayenne pepper. Cook for 4 minutes or until thickened. Add the soup, green onions and parsley. Cook for about 2 minutes. Discard the bay leaves and serve over the rice. Serves 4.

Cornflake-Crusted Shrimp with Pineapple Beurre Blanc

Pineapple Beurre Blanc
1 cup pineapple juice
1/4 cup lime juice
1/2 cup chopped shallots
2 tablespoons chopped fresh garlic
1/4 cup whipping cream

1 cup (2 sticks) unsalted butter,
    cut into small pieces
Salt and pepper to taste

Cornflake-Crusted Shrimp
12 large shrimp, peeled, deveined
    and butterflied

1 cup all-purpose flour
2 eggs, beaten
2 cups cornflake crumbs
Olive oil

For the beurre blanc, combine the pineapple juice, lime juice, shallots and garlic in a saucepan. Cook until reduced and thickened. Reduce the heat to very low. Whisk in the cream and butter. Cook just until the butter melts, moving the saucepan on and off the heat to keep the sauce warm but not hot, whisking constantly. Season with salt and pepper.

For the shrimp, flatten the shrimp slightly. Dip the shrimp in the flour and then in the eggs. Coat with the cornflake crumbs. Fry in olive oil in a skillet until golden brown; drain. Arrange three shrimp on each serving plate and drizzle with beurre blanc. Serves 4.

Linguini and Shrimp with Lemon Butter Sauce

16 ounces linguini or pasta
   of choice
Salt to taste
1 teaspoon olive oil
1 pound shrimp
1 cup (2 sticks) butter

1/4 cup fresh lemon juice
4 teaspoons Worcestershire sauce
1 teaspoon salt
2 tablespoons chopped shallots
6 garlic cloves, minced
2 tablespoons white wine
1/8 teaspoon red pepper flakes

Zest of 1 lemon
1/2 teaspoon black pepper
2 tablespoons chopped
   flat-leaf parsley
Freshly grated Parmesan cheese
   to taste

Pasta Tips

Use a large pot of water to cook pasta quickly and evenly and add a generous amount of salt to the water after it reaches a boil to replace the salt lost from the pasta as it cooks. Stir dried pasta immediately after adding it to the water and occasionally during cooking to prevent sticking. Cook al dente, tender but still chewy. Drain the pasta reserving some of its starchy cooking water to add to sauces if thickening is desired. Serve cooked pasta immediately. If it must sit, tossing lightly with olive oil will prevent sticking.

Cook the pasta in boiling salted water in a saucepan using the package directions; drain. Toss the pasta with the olive oil in a bowl to prevent the strands from sticking. Peel and devein the shrimp, leaving the tails intact.

Combine the butter, lemon juice, Worcestershire sauce and 1 teaspoon salt in a large skillet. Cook over medium heat until the butter melts. Add the shallots and garlic and cook for 2 minutes. Stir in the wine and red pepper flakes. Add the shrimp.

Cook for 5 minutes or until the shrimp turn pink. Add the pasta, lemon zest and black pepper and toss to combine. Season with salt to taste. Add the parsley and mix well. Mound on a serving platter and sprinkle with cheese. Serve immediately. Serves 4 to 6.

Photograph for this recipe on facing page.

Pasta Puttanesca

1 tablespoon olive oil
3 or 4 anchovy fillets (optional)
1/2 cup kalamata olives, chopped
2 tablespoons capers, drained
   and chopped

1 tablespoon minced fresh garlic
1 teaspoon crushed hot red
   pepper flakes
5 or 6 tomatoes, seeded and
   finely chopped

2 tablespoons fresh basil, chiffonade
16 ounces angel hair pasta
Salt and pepper to taste
3/4 cup (3 ounces) shredded
   Parmesan cheese

*T*his recipe requires 1 hour standing time. Heat the olive oil in a skillet until hot and add the anchovies. Cook for about 2 minutes or until the anchovies dissolve into the oil. Stir in the olives, capers, garlic and red pepper flakes. Cook for 1 to 2 minutes, stirring constantly. Combine the olive mixture with the tomatoes and basil in a bowl and mix well. Let stand at room temperature for 1 hour. Cook the pasta using the package directions until al dente; drain. Add to the tomato mixture and toss to combine. Season with salt and pepper. Sprinkle with the cheese. Serves 4 to 6.

Photograph for this recipe on facing page.

*O*ur dining table is a gorgeous thing with a golden glow and the scent of honey. She started out life over a century ago as part of a barn near my Dad's place in Blanco. My son and his grandfather crafted her for me. Her first dining room to preside in was our farm in Fayette County, arriving the day after we closed on the property. Though she helped out with Thanksgiving, Christmas, and several birthdays, she didn't make it 'til Easter. The house, being an octagarian herself, resented her presence, feeling the table was an upstart.

I moved the lovely lady to our Harris County home. Since the family settled there in the 1850s, we felt she would be able to hold her own. After all, she was the family Dining Table. Though she looked diminutive in the large room, it's here that she truly began to become part of the family. She presided over everything from pizza to chateaubriand with equal grace. By the time we moved to Jim Hogg County, I had to bring her along. We could not leave a part of our family behind. She was a perfect fit for the house built in the 1930s for the eccentric Ranch Foreman for what was once one of Texas' largest ranches. Having no kitchen table to compete with, she holds court over everything. She hears how great the quail crop is this year, how many points the trophy buck is, and who's winning the domino hand.

Though I'm back in our Harris County home, she remains at the ranch. A larger, less personable table resides in the dining room here. One day when my husband retires, I'm planning on moving her back home to be my desk. She, however, is not quite ready to give up her reign at the ranch. —D. Schiel

Creamy Artichoke Lasagna

Creamy Basil Cheese Sauce

1 cup chicken broth

1/4 cup all-purpose flour

1 tablespoon olive oil

1 garlic clove, minced

2 cups cream

1/2 cup loosely packed fresh
  basil, chiffonade

3/4 cup (3 ounces) finely shredded
  Parmesan cheese

Salt and pepper to taste

Artichoke Lasagna

2 tablespoons olive oil

2 cups finely chopped
  yellow onions

3 (any size) cans
  artichokes, drained

1/2 cup pine nuts, toasted

3 garlic cloves, minced

3 cups ricotta cheese

1/2 cup loosely packed fresh
  basil, chiffonade

1 egg, beaten

1 1/2 teaspoons salt

2 cups (8 ounces) shredded
  mozzarella cheese

3/4 cup (3 ounces) finely shredded
  Parmesan cheese

16 ounces lasagna noodles

1/4 cup pine nuts, toasted

*P*reheat the oven to 350 degrees.

For the sauce, pour the broth into a bowl. Add the flour gradually, stirring constantly until blended. Heat the olive oil in a saucepan over medium heat. Add the garlic and cook until the garlic is tender but not brown. Stir in the flour mixture and cream. Cook until the mixture is thickened and bubbly. Remove from the heat. Stir in the basil and cheese. Season with salt and pepper.

For the lasagna, heat the olive oil in a sauté pan over medium heat. Add the onions and sauté until tender. Stir in the artichokes, 1/2 cup pine nuts and the garlic. Cook for 8 to 10 minutes or until the artichokes are tender, stirring frequently. Combine the artichoke mixture, ricotta cheese, basil, egg and salt in a bowl and mix well. Mix the mozzarella cheese and Parmesan cheese in a bowl.

Spread about 1 cup of the sauce over the bottom of an ungreased shallow 3-quart baking dish. Layer with one-fourth of the noodles, half the artichoke mixture, one-third of the remaining noodles and half the remaining sauce. Sprinkle with half the mozzarella cheese mixture. Layer with half the remaining noodles, the remaining artichoke mixture and half the remaining sauce. Top with the remaining noodles, remaining sauce and remaining mozzarella cheese mixture.

Spray one side of a sheet of foil with nonstick cooking spray. Place the foil sprayed side down over the lasagna to prevent the cheese from sticking to the foil. Bake for 30 to 40 minutes. Remove the foil and bake for 10 minutes or until the edges are bubbly and the top is light brown. Sprinkle with 1/4 cup pine nuts. Let stand for 15 minutes before serving. Serves 12.

Shrimp and Asparagus Risotto

8 ounces fresh asparagus
8 cups chicken broth
2 tablespoons extra-virgin olive oil
1/2 cup chopped yellow onion
2 cups carnaroli or arborio rice
1/2 cup dry white wine
18 to 24 shrimp, peeled
   and deveined

1 1/2 cups (6 ounces) grated
   Parmesan cheese
1/2 cup (1 stick) butter, cut into
   small pieces
Salt and pepper to taste
1 cup chopped tomatoes (optional)
Chopped fresh parsley (optional)

Snap off the woody ends of the asparagus spears and discard. Cut the spears into 1-inch pieces. Bring the broth to a simmer in a saucepan over low heat; maintain the simmer. Heat the olive oil in a saucepan over medium heat. Add the onion and cook for 3 minutes or until the onion is tender. Stir in the rice and cook for 1 minute. Mix in the wine.

Add 1/2 cup of the warm broth and cook until the liquid is absorbed, stirring constantly. Repeat the process until 4 cups of the warm broth have been added, cooking until the liquid is absorbed after each addition and stirring frequently to prevent the rice from sticking.

Add the asparagus and shrimp to the remaining broth. Cook for 2 minutes or until the shrimp turn pink. Remove the asparagus and shrimp using a slotted spoon and add to the rice mixture.

Add the remaining broth 1/2 cup at a time until the desired creaminess is reached; some of the broth may remain. Stir in the cheese, butter, salt and pepper. Cook until the cheese and butter melt. Spoon the risotto into a serving bowl and garnish with the tomatoes and parsley. Serves 6.

Baked Stuffed Chiles Rellenos

3 (7-ounce) cans whole green
    chiles, drained (about 6 chiles)
1/2 to 1 cup finely chopped onion
1/2 teaspoon chopped garlic
2 tablespoons olive oil

3 cups (12 ounces) shredded
    Mexican Cheddar cheese
1 rotisserie chicken, shredded
    (optional)
1/2 cup milk
1/4 cup cream
2 eggs

2 teaspoons chopped cilantro
Salt and pepper to taste
1 cup (4 ounces) shredded
    Mexican Cheddar cheese
Green Tabasco sauce to taste
1 bottle salsa
Sour cream (optional)

Preheat the oven to 375 degrees. Cut a slit in the chiles lengthwise and lay flat. Discard the seeds. Sauté the onion and garlic in the olive oil in a skillet until the onion is tender. Stir in 3 cups cheese and the chicken. Fill each chile with equal portions of the cheese mixture and roll to enclose the filling.

Arrange the chiles seam side down in a greased 9×9-inch baking dish. Whisk the milk, cream, eggs, cilantro, salt and pepper in a bowl until combined. Pour over the chiles. Sprinkle with 1 cup cheese and drizzle with Tabasco sauce.

Bake for 35 to 40 minutes or until puffed, brown and firm. Heat the salsa in a saucepan and spoon over the top. Garnish with sour cream. Substitute fresh roasted Hatch chiles for the green chiles when in season. Double the recipe and freeze before baking for future use. Serves 4.

Photograph for this recipe on facing page.

Like most families, we celebrate with food and friends; so the tables in our home are well utilized. We celebrate many occasions in our home, even the loss of a tooth. Even when we are not hosting birthdays, wedding showers, or baby showers, our home stays busy. The kitchen table is the place where the boys do their homework and school projects (and the three-year-old does her arts and crafts). The table is usually decorated to fit the season. My husband made the tabletop, it has a lot of marks from the kids, so we may refinish it, but we will never get rid of that special table! The dining room table, though used much less, is a haven for dinner club, when we have other couples over and prepare a nice dinner (adults only). Reflecting on these celebrations, I realize now why we are staying in our home and remodeling. There are just too many great memories!
—S. Burchett

The Grill

"Throw it on the grill!" is a common sentiment, met with great enthusiasm and anticipation from family and guests alike, in the course of our outdoor-living style. Texans love to eat, drink, and play outdoors. Mild winters, early springs, extended summers, and late falls offer ample opportunity to throw something on the grill and entertain friends and family. Entire meals can be served straight from the grill to tables set up on the deck or patio. Not only does grilling satisfy taste buds and save us clean-up time, it also allows us to relax and enjoy time with our loved ones in our second living area, the backyard.

"A man can be short and dumpy and getting bald but if he has fire, women will like him."

—Mae West

Roquefort-Crusted Beef Tenderloin with Red Wine Sauce and Vegetables

Red Wine Sauce
8 cups (12-inch) cubes beef shanks
1/2 cup chopped shallots
6 garlic cloves, unpeeled and cut into halves
1 tablespoon clarified butter
5 cups red wine
5 cups veal stock
1 tablespoon butter

Vegetables
15 shallots
1 1/2 tablespoons clarified butter
1 1/2 teaspoons cracked pepper
Kosher salt to taste
2 parsnips, cut into 1/2×2-inch batons
2 carrots, cut into 1/4×2-inch julienne pieces
25 (3-inch) asparagus spears

Beef Tenderloin
6 ounces Roquefort cheese, crumbled
1/4 cup (1/2 stick) unsalted butter
2 ounces bread crumbs
1 tablespoon fresh thyme leaves, finely chopped
5 (10-ounce) beef tenderloin steaks
Kosher salt and freshly ground pepper to taste
1/3 cup Dijon mustard
1 to 2 bunches watercress

This recipe requires 8 hours of refrigeration. Preheat the oven to 375 degrees. Preheat the grill.

For the sauce, combine the beef shanks, shallots, garlic and clarified butter in a large roasting pan and mix well. Roast for 30 minutes, stirring every 10 minutes. Remove the beef mixture to a large stockpot, reserving the pan drippings. Reduce the oven temperature to 350 degrees. Add 3 1/2 cups of the wine to the beef mixture.

Heat the remaining 1 1/2 cups wine with the reserved pan drippings, scraping the bottom of the pan to dislodge any brown bits. Add the wine mixture to the stockpot and mix well. Bring to a rapid simmer.

Simmer for 1 hour or until the liquid is reduced to 1 to 1 1/2 cups. Stir in the stock. Simmer for about 1 1/2 hours. Chill for 8 to 10 hours. Skim any fat from the surface of the sauce. Simmer the sauce until reduced to the desired consistency. Add the butter gradually, whisking constantly until blended. Cover to keep warm.

For the vegetables, sauté the shallots in the clarified butter in a large heavy ovenproof skillet for 2 to 3 minutes or until tender. Add the pepper and salt and sauté for 2 minutes. Roast in the oven for 20 minutes.

Bring a large saucepan of lightly salted water to a boil. Add the parsnips and boil for 2 minutes. Add the carrots and boil for 2 minutes. Add the asparagus and boil for 2 minutes. Drain the vegetables and mix with the shallots. Cover to keep warm.

For the tenderloin, combine the cheese, butter, bread crumbs and thyme in a mixing bowl. Beat with a mixer fitted with a paddle attachment at medium speed for 2 minutes. Scrape the side of the bowl with a rubber spatula and beat for 2 minutes longer.

Season the steaks with salt and pepper. Brush each steak with 1/2 tablespoon of the Dijon mustard. Grill over hot coals for 3 minutes and then turn the steaks to create a crosshatch pattern. Grill for 3 minutes and turn the steaks. Grill for 3 minutes longer for medium-rare. You may sear the steaks in a hot sauté pan and finish in a preheated 400-degree oven, if desired.

Arrange the steaks on a baking sheet and spread each steak with 2 ounces of the cheese mixture. Broil until the cheese melts and the topping is light brown. Let the steaks stand in a warm, but not hot, area for 3 minutes. To serve, spoon 1/4 cup of the sauce in the center of each of five heated serving plates. Spoon 3 ounces of the vegetables at the 3 o'clock position on the plates and place four stems of the watercress at the 12 o'clock position. Arrange the steaks over the sauce and serve immediately. Serves 5.

Courtesy of James Nuetzi, Executive Chef, The Capital Grille

My relationship with my kitchen table began some twenty years ago when my mother and I went shopping for a new desk for me. She recommended finding something I could use in the future, so we chose a new pine farm table. In high school that table served me well as a place for homework. When I got my first apartment, I ate many a meal on it. My table was there when my husband cooked me our first meal together. It has traveled with me to many different cities and states. Now several children later it serves as the hub for the family for homework, crafts, and a few meals. Although it doesn't look the same with the worn finish, divots, and permanent marker scars, it still gets the job done just as well and has more stories to tell. —L. Kamasz

Tasty Texas Fajitas

1 (4-ounce) can chopped green
  chiles, drained
1/2 cup beer
1/2 cup pineapple juice
1/4 cup soy sauce

1/4 cup vegetable oil
1/4 cup fresh lime juice
1 tablespoon teriyaki sauce
1 teaspoon hot pepper sauce
1/2 teaspoon ground cumin
1/4 teaspoon freshly
  cracked pepper

1 (1- to 2-pound) flank steak
2 cups thin strips yellow onions
2 poblano chiles, seeded and sliced
  into strips
6 to 9 flour tortillas

This recipe requires 6 hours of refrigeration. Preheat the grill on medium. Mix the green chiles, beer, pineapple juice, soy sauce, oil, lime juice, teriyaki sauce, hot sauce, cumin and pepper in a bowl and pour into a large sealable plastic bag. Add the steak, onions and poblano chiles and seal tightly. Shake to coat.

Marinate in the refrigerator for 6 to 24 hours, turning occasionally. Drain, reserving the steak, onions and poblano chiles. Place the onions and poblano chiles on a double layer of heavy-duty foil. Seal tightly to enclose the onions and poblano chiles, leaving enough space to allow steam to build. Stack the tortillas and wrap in a double layer of heavy-duty foil.

Place the steak and the foil packet of the onions and poblano chiles on the grill rack. Grill for 10 minutes and turn the steak. Place the wrapped tortillas on the grill rack. Grill for 8 to 10 minutes or until the steak is the desired degree of doneness. Remove the steak to a platter and let stand for about 5 minutes. Remove the tortillas and vegetables from the grill.

Cut the steak diagonally against the grain into thin strips. Divide the steak, onions and poblano chiles among the tortillas. Add toppings such as salsa, avocados, tomatoes and sour cream, if desired. Roll to enclose the filling and serve immediately. Makes 6 to 9 fajitas.

Grilled Branzino Agrume

Blood Orange Agrume

Sections of 6 (or more)
blood oranges
5 tablespoons extra-virgin olive oil
1/2 cup fresh blood orange juice or
fresh orange juice
1 1/2 tablespoons chopped
Italian parsley
1 1/2 tablespoons chopped
fresh mint
Salt and pepper to taste

Grilled Branzino

1 (16-ounce) branzino or other
sea bass
2 tablespoons extra-virgin olive oil
2 tablespoons chopped
Italian parsley
1 tablespoon minced garlic
Oregano to taste
Salt and pepper to taste

Preheat the grill.

For the agrume, cut along either side of each orange section to remove the membrane.
Cut the sections into 1/4-inch pieces and place in a stainless steel bowl; squeeze the pieces
to release the juice. Stir in the olive oil, orange juice, parsley and mint. The sauce should be
fairly chunky. Add additional orange sections if the sauce is not chunky. Season with salt
and pepper.

For the branzino, have the butcher remove the scales and head and butterfly the
branzino. Remove the bones, leaving the skin intact. Mix the olive oil, parsley, garlic and
oregano in a small bowl. Coat the flesh side of the branzino with the olive oil mixture.
Season with salt and pepper. Spray the flesh side lightly with nonstick cooking spray.
Arrange the branzino flesh side down on the grill rack.

Grill for 2 minutes and turn 90 degrees; do not turn over. Grill for about 2 to
3 minutes or until cooked through. Arrange the branzino skin side down on a serving
platter and top with the agrume. Serve immediately. Serves 3.

Courtesy of Tony Vallone, Tony's

Rib-Eye Steaks with Peppercorn Brandy Sauce

2 (16-ounce) rib-eye steaks,
    about 1 inch thick
1 teaspoon kosher salt
Freshly cracked pepper to taste
2 tablespoons butter
4 garlic cloves, minced
1 shallot, minced
2 tablespoons unsalted butter

3/4 cup brandy
1/2 cup beef or veal demi-glace
1/4 to 1/2 cup heavy cream
1 1/2 teaspoons green peppercorns
    in brine, drained
2 tablespoons unsalted butter
Kosher salt to taste

Season the steaks with 1 teaspoon salt and pepper. Heat a heavy skillet over high heat until hot and add 2 tablespoons butter and the steaks. Sear the steaks for 1 minute or until the blood rises in the uncooked surface. Turn the steaks and sear the other side. Reduce the heat and cook for about 10 minutes or until the desired degree of doneness. Remove to a platter and cover with foil to keep warm. You may grill the steaks if desired.

Sauté the garlic and shallot in 2 tablespoons butter in a skillet. Add the brandy and bring to a boil. Reduce the heat and simmer until the mixture is reduced by three-fourths. Stir in the accumulated steak juices, demi-glace and cream.

Simmer until the mixture is reduced by one-third. Stir in the peppercorns. Whisk in 2 tablespoons butter and season with salt to taste and pepper. Simmer just until heated through. Slice the steaks as desired and divide evenly among two to four serving plates. Spoon the peppercorn sauce over the steaks. Serve with Jalapeño Cheddar Gratin Potatoes on page 116 if desired. Serves 2 to 4.

Photograph for this recipe on facing page.

Did You Know?

A steak knife should never be placed on the table at the beginning of the meal. It should be placed only when the meat course is served.

Korean Beef with Cilantro Sauce

Cilantro Sauce

3/4 cup loosely packed
  cilantro leaves
1/3 cup olive oil
3 tablespoons soy sauce
1 1/2 tablespoons sesame oil
1 tablespoon fresh lime juice
1 1/2 teaspoons minced garlic
1 teaspoon minced seeded
  serrano chile

Korean Beef and Assembly

3/4 cup soy sauce
3 tablespoons sugar
2 tablespoons sherry vinegar
1 1/2 tablespoons sesame oil
1 1/2 tablespoons minced garlic
1 teaspoon red pepper flakes
4 boneless strip steaks, at least
  1-inch thick

This recipe requires 1 hour of refrigeration. Preheat the grill on medium.

For the sauce, combine the cilantro, olive oil, soy sauce, sesame oil, lime juice, garlic and serrano chile in a bowl and mix well.

For the beef, combine the soy sauce, sugar, vinegar, sesame oil, garlic and red pepper flakes in a large plastic container and mix until the sugar dissolves. You may pour the marinade into a large sealable plastic bag at this time, if desired. Add the steaks and turn to coat. Marinate, covered, in the refrigerator for 1 hour or longer, turning occasionally; drain.

Grill the steaks for 3 to 4 minutes per side for medium-rare or to the desired degree of doneness. Let stand for about 5 minutes. Slice the steaks diagonally against the grain into 3/4- to 1-inch strips. Arrange one steak on each of four serving plates and drizzle with the sauce. The steaks may be seared in a sauté pan and baked in a preheated 425-degree oven to the desired degree of doneness if a grill is not available. If desired serve over Sautéed Sugar Snap Peas on page 119. Serves 4.

Photograph for this recipe on facing page.

1 to 2 tablespoons vegetable oil
2 pounds 85% lean ground beef
1 tablespoon Worcestershire sauce
1 tablespoon Dijon mustard
1 1/2 teaspoons ground pepper

4 thick slices bacon, crisp-cooked
    and crumbled
4 ounces Roquefort
    cheese, crumbled
1 teaspoon fresh thyme leaves

4 hamburger buns or onion rolls,
    split and toasted
1 ripe tomato, sliced
1 red onion, sliced
4 large crisp lettuce leaves

This recipe requires refrigeration. Lightly coat the grill rack with the oil. Preheat the grill on medium-high. Combine the ground beef, Worcestershire sauce, Dijon mustard and pepper in a bowl and mix gently until combined. Be careful not to overmix or the hamburgers will be tough. Divide the ground beef mixture into eight equal portions. Flatten each portion into a round patty.

Mix the bacon, cheese and thyme in a bowl until combined. Spread equal portions of the cheese mixture on four of the patties to within 1 inch of the edges. Top with the remaining patties, pinching the edges to seal in the cheese mixture. Arrange the patties on a baking sheet and cover. Chill, covered, in the refrigerator.

Arrange the patties on the grill rack and grill for about 6 to 10 minutes per side or until cooked through and easily removed from the grill rack with a spatula. Serve immediately on the toasted buns with the tomato, onion and lettuce. These burgers can also be made into small sliders. Serves 4.

Photograph for this recipe on facing page.

In the immediate days after Hurricane Ike devastated Galveston and much of the Gulf Coast area, we, like most, were without power. It was one of those early days that we drove to the home of a friend for dinner. Our friend had a gas stovetop, a gas grill, and a smoker. We took meat—a lot of meat. When we arrived, the house was full of other friends who had also brought a variety of defrosted meat and other items that would not survive another day without refrigeration. We opened bottles of wine and cooked. Every table and countertop available in the kitchen area was covered with food! We gathered around the large kitchen island, lit by flashlights and lanterns and celebrated—celebrated for the damage that did not occur, celebrated that we had survived, and celebrated just being together.   —Y. Williams

Greek Burgers with Tzatziki Sauce

Tzatziki Sauce

1 small cucumber
1 1/2 cups yogurt
1/2 cup crumbled Greek
    feta cheese
1 garlic clove, minced

Grilled Eggplant (optional)

3 tablespoons white wine vinegar
1/2 teaspoon oregano
1/2 teaspoon salt
1/4 teaspoon pepper
1/4 cup olive oil
1 large eggplant, cut into
    1/2-inch rounds

Lamb Burgers and Assembly

2 pounds ground lamb
3/4 cup mint leaves
1 1/2 tablespoons ground cumin
Salt and pepper to taste
1 tablespoon vegetable oil
6 small pitas or miniature
    hamburger buns
3 cups shredded romaine

*T*his recipe requires 1 hour of refrigeration. Prepare a grill for medium direct heat.

For the sauce, peel, seed and chop the cucumber. Combine the cucumber, yogurt, cheese and garlic in a bowl and mix well. Chill, covered, for 1 hour.

For the eggplant, mix the vinegar, oregano, salt and pepper in a bowl. Add the olive oil gradually, whisking constantly until thickened and blended. Arrange the eggplant in a 9×13-inch baking dish. Add the oil mixture and turn to coat. Grill the eggplant over direct heat for 3 minutes per side or until tender. Remove to a platter and cover to keep warm.

For the burgers, combine the lamb, mint, cumin, salt and pepper in a bowl and mix well. Divide the lamb mixture into six equal portions. Shape each portion into a patty. Brush the grill rack with the oil. Grill the patties for 4 minutes per side, turning once.

Separate the pitas and arrange on the grill rack. Toast lightly over indirect heat. Layer each pita bottom with equal portions of the romaine, burger, a generous amount of the sauce, eggplant slice and a pita top in the order listed. Serve immediately. Serves 6.

Photograph for this recipe on page 187.

Wood-Grilled Pork Tenderloin with Peach Barbeque Sauce

Peach Barbeque Sauce

8 ounces smoked bacon, chopped,
    or 1 ham hock

1 cup coarsely chopped smoked
    or grilled onion

4 smoked or grilled garlic
    cloves, chopped

2 arbol chiles, stemmed

2 cups coarsely chopped fresh or
    dried peaches

1 tablespoon cracked pepper

2 cups fresh orange juice

2 tablespoons Worcestershire sauce

2 cups ketchup

6 dashes of Tabasco sauce

Juice of 2 lemons

2 teaspoons kosher salt

Pork Tenderloin

8 (8-ounce) portions pork
    tenderloin, fat and
    silver skin removed

6 tablespoons olive oil

2 tablespoons kosher salt

2 tablespoons cracked pepper

1 tablespoon granulated garlic

Crispy fried onions (optional)

Preheat the grill or a charbroiler.

For the sauce, cook the bacon in a small saucepan over medium heat until crisp. Add the onion and garlic and sauté until the onion is caramelized. Add the arbol chiles and cook until the chiles begin to brown. Stir in the peaches and pepper. Deglaze the saucepan with the orange juice and Worcestershire sauce, stirring with a wooden spoon to loosen any brown bits.

Cook just until the sauce begins to thicken. Stir in the ketchup and reduce the heat to low. Cook for 15 minutes, stirring occasionally. Mix in the Tabasco sauce, lemon juice and salt. Strain into a bowl, discarding the solids.

For the pork, rub the tenderloin with the olive oil and sprinkle with the salt, pepper and garlic. Grill the pork over an open flame to the desired degree of doneness; medium-rare is preferred. Slice the pork as desired and arrange on a serving platter. Garnish with crispy fried onions. Serve with the sauce and Bourbon Cream Corn on page 111. Serves 8.

Courtesy of Kent Rathbun, Executive Chef/Partner, Jasper's

Peaches

Texas produces firm, ripe peaches with a bright red blush. A cream to yellow background indicates ripeness and flavor. Cling peaches generally ripen first, followed by semi-freestones and freestones. Texas peaches are ripened on the tree, which assures buyers receive the highest quality, sweetest peaches possible.

Grilled Chicken with Mango and Avocado Salsa

Grilled Chicken

12 (4-ounce) boneless skinless
    chicken breasts
1 1/2 cups white wine
Juice of 1 lemon
Juice of 1 orange
2 tablespoons vegetable oil
2 tablespoons black peppercorns
1 tablespoon fresh rosemary

2 teaspoons chopped fresh basil
3 bay leaves (optional)
2 tablespoons vegetable oil

Mango and Avocado Salsa

3 mangoes, chopped
6 tablespoons finely chopped
    green bell pepper
6 tablespoons finely chopped
    red bell pepper

2 tablespoons chopped
    cilantro leaves
1 tablespoon ground pepper
1 tablespoon olive oil
2 teaspoons chopped chives
2 teaspoons salt
6 tablespoons minced onion
1/4 cup sugar
3 tablespoons Champagne vinegar
1 large avocado, chopped

*T*his recipe requires 4 hours of refrigeration. Preheat the grill on medium.

For the chicken, place the chicken in a shallow dish. Mix the wine, lemon juice, orange juice, 2 tablespoons oil, the peppercorns, rosemary, basil and bay leaves in a bowl and pour over the chicken, turning to coat. Marinate, covered, in the refrigerator for 4 to 6 hours, turning occasionally; drain. Coat the chicken with 2 tablespoons oil. Grill for 10 to 12 minutes or until cooked through and firm to the touch.

For the salsa, combine the mangoes, bell peppers, cilantro, pepper, olive oil, chives and salt in a heatproof bowl and mix well. Bring the onion, sugar and vinegar to a boil in a small saucepan and pour over the mango mixture, tossing to coat. Stir in the avocado just before serving. Season as desired. Serve over the chicken. The salsa is also good served as a dip with chips. Serves 6.

Photograph for this recipe on facing page.

Pollo Bahia (Coconut Grilled Chicken with Tomato and Hearts of Palm)

1 teaspoon olive oil
1 (6-ounce) chicken breast
1/4 cup chicken stock
1/2 cup lemon juice

1/4 cup coconut milk
1/4 cup (1/2 stick) butter, chopped
2 ounces hearts of palm, sliced
2 ounces tomato, chopped
1 ounce cilantro, chopped

1 cup basmati rice, cooked
1 ounce green onion (optional)
1 ounce sesame seeds, toasted
  (optional)

Preheat the grill on medium-high. Drizzle the olive oil over the chicken and season as desired. Grill for 6 to 8 minutes per side or until cooked through. Remove to a platter and cover to keep warm. Bring the stock and lemon juice to a boil in a saucepan. Boil until reduced by three-fourths. Stir in the coconut milk. Add the butter gradually, whisking constantly until blended. Stir in the hearts of palm, tomato and cilantro. Pour one ladleful of the coconut sauce into a shallow bowl and add the rice. Arrange the chicken over the rice and drizzle with the remaining coconut sauce. Garnish with the green onion and sesame seeds. Serves 1.

Courtesy of Michael J. Cordúa, Executive Chef and Owner, Cordúa Restaurants-Américas Woodlands

Perfect Steamed Rice

In a saucepan bring four cups of water to a boil. Add one teaspoon sea salt and two cups long-grain white rice. Reduce the heat to low, cover, and simmer for about twenty minutes or until the water is absorbed and the rice is tender. Remove from the heat, cover, and let stand for five minutes. Fluff with a fork and serve.

Pena Pancetta-Wrapped Quail

8 quail breasts, deboned
Salt and pepper to taste

10 ounces Monterey Jack cheese,
  cut into 1/2-inch cubes

1 cup julienned seeded
  jalapeño peppers
16 slices pancetta or bacon

Prepare a charcoal grill for medium heat. Sprinkle both sides of the quail with salt and pepper. Place three cheese cubes on each quail breast and top each with two jalapeño pepper strips. Wrap each quail breast tightly with two slices of the pancetta and secure with moistened wooden picks. Grill the quail over hot coals for 30 minutes, turning frequently until the pancetta is crisp. Or, broil on low for 15 minutes, turning frequently. Increase the heat to high to crisp the pancetta. Oven-broiling will not yield similar crispness of the pancetta. Serves 4.

Photograph for this recipe on page 175.

Zip Vegetables

Zip Sauce
1 cup vegetable oil
1/2 cup soy sauce
3 tablespoons honey
2 tablespoons minced garlic
2 teaspoons fresh lemon juice

2 tablespoons Worcestershire
    sauce

Grilled Vegetables
1 zucchini
1 yellow squash

1 eggplant
2 thick carrots
1 red or yellow bell pepper
1 bunch asparagus
3 Roma tomatoes, cut into halves

This recipe requires 2 hours of refrigeration. Preheat the grill on medium.

For the sauce, combine the oil, soy sauce, honey, garlic, lemon juice and Worcestershire sauce in a food processor. Process until blended. Store, covered, in the refrigerator for up to 1 week. If the sauce separates, shake or reprocess until emulsified. The sauce can also be used as a marinade for chicken or fish.

For the vegetables, cut the zucchini, yellow squash, eggplant and carrots diagonally into 1/3-inch slices. Slice off the top and bottom of the bell pepper and discard. Remove the seeds. Cut the bell pepper into triangles or slice as desired. Snap off the woody ends of the asparagus spears; the spears should be 4 to 5 inches long. Place the vegetables in separate sealable plastic bags or plastic containers. Cover the vegetables with the sauce and seal tightly. Shake to coat. Marinate in the refrigerator for 2 to 12 hours, turning occasionally.

Line a baking sheet with baking parchment. Grill the zucchini, yellow squash, eggplant, carrots, bell pepper and tomatoes on the grill rack until tender. Grill the asparagus for 4 to 7 minutes depending on the thickness of the spears. Remove the vegetables to the prepared baking sheet. Serve on a platter lined with kale. Butternut squash, sweet potatoes, mushrooms or the vegetable of your choice may be substituted. Serves 6.

Photograph for this recipe on page 175.

Measuring Honey

When measuring sticky ingredients such as honey, spray a small amount of nonstick spray into the measuring utensil before pouring the ingredient inside—it should slide right out.

Cedar-Planked Salmon with Jalapeño Cream Sauce

Salmon

1 (1½-pound) salmon fillet
1 tablespoon olive oil
2 garlic cloves, minced
1 tablespoon chopped cilantro
½ teaspoon salt
½ teaspoon white pepper

Jalapeño Cream Sauce

1½ teaspoons butter
2 cups finely chopped
  yellow onions
6 white mushrooms,
  finely chopped
6 small fresh jalapeño peppers,
  seeded and finely chopped

1 cup sauvignon blanc
1½ cups heavy whipping cream
Salt and freshly cracked black
  pepper to taste
Rice pilaf or hot cooked wild rice

Soak one cedar plank using the manufacturers' directions. Preheat the grill or oven to 375 degrees.

For the salmon, arrange the salmon on the soaked plank and brush with the olive oil. Rub with the garlic and cilantro. Sprinkle with the salt and white pepper. Grill for 20 to 30 minutes or until the salmon flakes easily. Do not overcook, as the salmon will continue to cook after it is removed from the grill. Or, bake in the oven until the salmon flakes easily. Place a baking sheet under the plank to catch any drippings.

For the sauce, melt the butter in a medium skillet over medium heat and add the onions, mushrooms and jalapeño peppers. Sauté until the butter is absorbed and the onions and mushrooms are tender. Add ½ cup of the wine and stir. Mix in ¾ cup of the cream, the salt and pepper. Bring to a low boil.

Cook until the mixture begins to thicken. Stir in the remaining ½ cup wine and the remaining ¾ cup cream. Bring to a low boil and cook until thickened to the desired consistency, stirring constantly. Remove from the heat. Purée using an immersion blender. Strain the sauce through a colander into a bowl, pressing the solids with a spoon; discard the solids. Season with salt and pepper. Add additional cream if a thinner consistency is desired.

Arrange equal portions of rice pilaf on each of three or four serving plates. Cut the salmon into three or four equal portions and arrange one portion on each serving of rice. Drizzle with the sauce and serve with fresh green beans. Store any leftover sauce in the refrigerator. It will cool into a thick paste, but reheats well in a double boiler. Serves 3 or 4.

Photograph for this recipe on facing page.

The Dessert Cart

There are few things in life greeted with such bated breath as the sight of desserts perfectly placed on the center table waiting for us to indulge. We share, with great excitement, thoughts on each before choosing the perfect dessert, even bartering with friends to get a taste of more than our own. When Europeans initially settled in our Texas coastal plain area, they brought a love for all things sweet. Today that love stands strong in every ounce of richness mixed into the grand finale of the meal. Dessert, the ultimate indulgence, is cherished and celebrates special moments, bite for bite.

> *"A compromise is the art of dividing a cake in such a way that everyone believes that he has got the biggest piece."*
>
> —Paul Gauguin

Sweet Georgia Cheesecake

1¹/₄ cups graham cracker crumbs
3 tablespoons sugar
¹/₂ cup (1 stick) butter, softened

32 ounces cream cheese, softened
4 eggs
1¹/₃ cups sugar

1 tablespoon vanilla extract
(optional)

This recipe requires 2¹/₂ hours refrigeration. Preheat the oven to 325 degrees. Mix the graham cracker crumbs and 3 tablespoons sugar in a bowl. Add the butter and mix with a fork until crumbly. Press the crumb mixture over the bottom and up the side of a 9-inch soufflé dish or ceramic baking dish.

Place the cream cheese in a mixing bowl. Add the eggs one at a time, mixing well after each addition and beating until the mixture is light and fluffy. Add 1¹/₃ cups sugar gradually, beating constantly until blended. Stir in the vanilla. Spoon the cream cheese mixture over the prepared layer.

Place the soufflé dish in a large baking pan. Add enough water to the baking pan to reach halfway up the side of the soufflé dish. Bake on the middle oven rack for 2 hours. Remove the soufflé dish from the water bath and place on a wire rack. Let stand until cool. Chill in the refrigerator for 2¹/₂ hours for a better release. Trim any brown crust from the top. Invert the soufflé dish onto a serving platter. Garnish as desired. Serve with your favorite chocolate sauce. If the vanilla is omitted, serve with raspberry coulis. Serves 8 to 10.

It was a Friday evening just short of a month before I was scheduled to quit my job in one city and join my boyfriend in a new city and start planning our wedding. We had purchased a house, so I was in town every weekend to help with renovations and visit with his family. On this particular Friday evening, dinner was a little different. It was after dessert, as were preparing to clear the table, that my husband announced to his parents that we had gotten married at the Justice of Peace's office that afternoon. His mom couldn't scoot around the large round table fast enough and climbed over the tabletop to hug me and say, "Finally!" That was a great moment!   —Y. Williams

Key Lime Cheesecake

1 recipe graham cracker crust
   (see recipe on page 200)
4 gelatin sheets

3 cups heavy whipping cream
1 1/8 pounds (17 ounces) cream
   cheese, softened for 2 hours

1 1/2 cups sugar
1/2 cup Key lime juice

This recipe requires 3 hours of refrigeration and 1 hour freezer time. Pat the graham cracker crumb mixture over the bottom and up the side of a springform pan. Soften the gelatin in a small amount of warm water in a bowl. Beat the cream in a mixing bowl until soft peaks form. Beat the cream cheese and sugar in a mixing bowl fitted with a paddle attachment at high speed for 3 minutes or until creamy. Add the Key lime juice and beat at medium speed until blended. Spoon 3 cups of the cream cheese mixture into a stainless steel bowl and fold in the gelatin. Mix in the remaining cream cheese mixture and fold in the whipped cream. Pipe the cream cheese mixture into the prepared pan. Chill, covered, for 3 to 4 hours. Freeze for 1 hour. If gelatin sheets are unavailable, you can dissolve 1 package unflavored gelatin in 1/4 cup boiling water. Dissolve and let cool. Serves 10 to 12.

Courtesy of James Nuetzi, Executive Chef, The Capital Grille

Manzanilla: Chamomile-Scented Crème Brûlée

4 cups whipping cream
2 ounces loose-leaf chamomile
   tea leaves

8 egg yolks
1 cup sugar

1 tablespoon vanilla extract
Sugar to taste

Preheat the oven to 300 degrees. Bring the cream to a simmer in a saucepan. Stir in the tea leaves and remove from the heat. Let stand, covered, for several minutes. Whisk the egg yolks and 1 cup sugar in a bowl until of a ribbon texture. Stir a small amount of the hot cream into the egg yolk mixture. Stir the egg yolk mixture into the hot cream. Add the vanilla and strain into an 8-quart container. Pour equal portions of the custard into four to six crème brûlée ramekins. Place the ramekins in a large baking pan. Add enough water to reach halfway up the sides of the ramekins and cover with foil. Bake for 1 hour or until a skewer inserted in the center of one of the custards comes out clean. Cool on a wire rack for 2 hours. Sprinkle the tops of the custards with sugar to taste. Caramelize the sugar using a kitchen torch. Serves 4 to 6.

Courtesy of Michael J. Cordúa, Executive Chef and Owner, Cordúa Restaurants-Américas Woodlands

Cappuccino Flan

1 cup sugar
1/2 cup water
Juice of 1/2 lemon
4 cups heavy whipping cream

1 fresh vanilla bean
8 egg yolks
1/2 cup sugar
1/4 cup Tuaca or Grand Marnier

2 tablespoons ground dark roasted
   espresso beans
Fresh berries (optional)
Sprigs of mint (optional)

Blackberries

In May and early June, wild blackberries are sold along Texas highways. Small plots of cultivated blackberries are also scattered throughout the state. In East Texas production has accelerated so much in recent years that blackberries are now available in grocery stores in major Texas cities. Research indicates that eating blackberries helps reduce cholesterol and the likelihood of certain cancers.

This recipe requires 3 hours of refrigeration. Preheat the oven to 350 degrees. Combine 1 cup sugar, the water and lemon juice in a 2-quart saucepan. Bring to a boil over high heat and boil until golden brown; do not stir. Remove from the heat and cool for 1 minute. Pour just enough of the caramel mixture into eight 6-ounce or six 8-ounce ceramic ramekins sprayed with nonstick cooking spray to cover the bottoms. Let stand until cool.

Pour the cream into a bowl. Split the vanilla bean lengthwise into halves and scrape the seeds into the cream; add the pod. Whisk the egg yolks and 1/2 cup sugar in a heatproof bowl until blended. Combine the cream mixture, liqueur and espresso in a saucepan. Cook over low heat for 5 minutes or until the mixture begins to release steam, stirring occasionally. Stir a small amount of the hot cream into the egg yolk mixture. Gradually stir the remaining hot cream into the egg yolk mixture, whisking constantly to prevent the eggs from curdling. Strain through a fine sieve into a bowl, discarding the solids. Pour into the prepared ramekins.

Place the ramekins in a baking pan. Add enough hot water to the baking pan to reach three-fourths up the sides of the ramekins. Bake on the lower oven rack for about 35 minutes for 6-ounce ramekins or 45 minutes for 8-ounce ramekins. Cover the ramekins with a piece of baking parchment sprayed with nonstick cooking spray if the tops begin to brown. Chill in the refrigerator for 3 hours or longer. Run a sharp knife around the edges of the ramekins and invert onto individual dessert plates. Garnish with fresh berries and sprigs of mint. Makes 8 (6-ounce) or 6 (8-ounce) flans.

Photograph for this recipe on facing page.

Tiramisu Even You Can Do

3/4 cup sugar
2/3 cup water
1 1/3 cups hot strong coffee
4 tablespoons amaretto
4 tablespoons hazelnut liqueur

16 ounces mascarpone cheese, softened
1/3 cup sugar
1 teaspoon vanilla extract
1 1/2 cups heavy whipping cream

3 (3-ounce) packages ladyfingers
1 tablespoon baking cocoa
Fresh raspberries (optional)
Bailey's Irish cream or any Irish cream liqueur (optional)

This recipe requires 4 hours of refrigeration. Bring 3/4 cup sugar and the water to a boil in a saucepan and boil until the sugar dissolves. Remove from the heat and let stand until cool. Stir in the coffee, amaretto and hazelnut liqueur.

Combine the cheese, 1/3 cup sugar and the vanilla in a bowl and mix well. Beat the cream in a chilled mixing bowl with chilled beaters at medium speed until soft peaks form. Fold 1/2 cup of the whipped cream into the cheese mixture. Fold in the remaining whipped cream.

Arrange half the ladyfingers in a square 2-quart baking dish. Brush with half the coffee syrup and spread with half the cheese mixture. Top with the remaining ladyfingers and brush with the remaining coffee syrup. Spread with the remaining cheese mixture and sprinkle with the baking cocoa. Chill, covered, for 4 to 24 hours. Garnish each serving with fresh raspberries and drizzle with Irish cream. Serves 16.

Chocolate Cream Shooters

1 (2-ounce) package European-style dark chocolate mousse mix

1 cup whipped cream
1 teaspoon instant coffee granules

10 Werther's Original hard candies, finely chopped
1/2 teaspoon garam masala

This recipe requires 2 hours of refrigeration. Prepare the mousse using the package directions. Combine the prepared mousse, 1/4 cup of the whipped cream and the coffee granules in a bowl and mix gently. Spoon the mousse mixture equally into four parfait glasses. Chill for 2 to 3 hours. Fold half the candies into the remaining 3/4 cup whipped cream in a bowl. Top each parfait with an equal portion of the whipped cream mixture. Mix the remaining candies and garam masala in a bowl. Sprinkle over the parfaits just before serving. Serves 4.

Photograph for this recipe on page 224.

White Chocolate Bread Pudding

Bread Pudding

1 to 1 1/2 loaves French bread, cut into 1/2-inch slices
15 egg yolks
1 cup sugar
1 tablespoon vanilla extract
1/2 teaspoon nutmeg
Pinch of salt
4 cups heavy cream
8 ounces white chocolate, chopped

White Chocolate Rum Sauce

3 egg yolks
1/4 cup sugar
2 cups heavy cream
4 to 8 ounces white chocolate, chopped
1 1/2 teaspoons vanilla extract
1/4 cup light rum

*T*his recipe requires 3 hours of refrigeration. Preheat the oven to 300 degrees.

For the pudding, layer the bread slices slightly overlapping in a 9×13-inch baking pan. Whisk the egg yolks in a double boiler over simmering water or in a stainless steel bowl over simmering water in a saucepan until blended. Stir in the sugar, vanilla, nutmeg and salt. Simmer the cream in a saucepan until bubbles appear around the edge. Stir a small amount of the hot cream into the egg yolk mixture. Add the remaining hot cream gradually, whisking constantly until blended to prevent the eggs from curdling. If the eggs do curdle, strain through a strainer to remove the lumps. Add the white chocolate to the egg mixture and cook for 2 minutes or until the chocolate melts. Pour over the bread slices. Chill, covered, for 3 hours or longer. Bake, covered with foil, for 1 to 1 1/2 hours or until set.

For the sauce, whisk the eggs and sugar together in a saucepan. Simmer the cream in a saucepan until bubbles appear around the edge of the pan. Remove from the heat. Stir a small amount of the hot cream into the egg mixture. Stir the remaining hot cream into the egg mixture. Cook until thickened, stirring occasionally. Stir in the white chocolate and vanilla. Cook until the chocolate melts. Stir in the rum. Drizzle the warm sauce over the bread pudding. Serves 10 to12.

Vanilla Pods

Vanilla pods are derived from the vanilla orchid and are grown in Central America, Mexico, and throughout the Asia Pacific islands. Less common than vanilla extract in the United States, vanilla pods are simple to use and have a much purer concentration of flavor than extract. Split the bean lengthwise with a kitchen knife, then scrape the tiny beans into your dish. This is a simple way to give a better vanilla flavor to your dishes.

Bread Pudding with Butterscotch Sauce

1 loaf French bread, cut into
    1-inch slices
3 1/2 cups hot water
2 cups sugar

1 (12-ounce) can evaporated milk
5 eggs
1 tablespoon vanilla extract
1/2 cup sugar
1 tablespoon cinnamon

1/2 cup (1 stick) butter
2 cups sugar
1 egg
1/4 cup Buttershots liqueur

Preheat the oven to 350 degrees. Arrange the bread slices in a single layer on a baking sheet and toast on both sides until light brown. Arrange the slices over the bottom of a 9×13-inch baking dish. Whisk the hot water, 2 cups sugar, the evaporated milk, 5 eggs and the vanilla in a bowl until blended. Pour over the bread slices and let stand for 5 minutes. Mix 1/2 cup sugar and the cinnamon in a small bowl and sprinkle over the top. Bake, covered with foil, for 45 to 50 minutes or until set.

Melt the butter in a saucepan and whisk in 2 cups sugar. Cook until bubbly, stirring occasionally. Remove from the heat and let stand until cool. Whisk 1 egg with the liqueur in a bowl until blended and stir into the butter mixture. Serve over the bread pudding. Serves 10 to 12.

Old-Fashioned Apple Crisp

3/4 cup packed brown sugar
3/4 cup all-purpose flour
1/2 cup granulated sugar
1/2 cup old-fashioned oats
1 teaspoon cinnamon

3/4 cup (1 1/2 sticks) butter,
    chilled and cut into pieces
6 Granny Smith apples, peeled
    and cut into 1/2-inch slices
    (about 2 1/4 pounds)

1/4 cup orange juice
1 tablespoon dark rum
1/2 teaspoon vanilla extract
1/4 cup chopped pecans
Vanilla ice cream (optional)

Preheat the oven to 325 degrees. Combine the brown sugar, flour, granulated sugar, oats and cinnamon in a bowl and mix well. Cut in the butter until crumbly.

Toss the apples and 1/2 cup of the crumb mixture together in a bowl. Spoon the apple mixture into a buttered 8×8-inch baking pan. Mix the orange juice, rum and vanilla in a bowl and drizzle over the apples. Toss the pecans with the remaining crumb mixture and sprinkle over the top. Bake for 40 to 45 minutes or until bubbly and the topping is light brown. Serve warm over vanilla ice cream. Serves 6.

Chocolate Raspberry Tarts

Short Dough
4 eggs
5 ounces (1¼ cups)
    confectioners' sugar
¼ cup (½ stick) unsalted butter
1 vanilla bean
¼ teaspoon baking
    powder, sifted

6½ ounces (1½ cups)
    all-purpose flour, sifted

Chocolate Filling
12 ounces high-quality semisweet
    chocolate
1¼ cups heavy whipping cream
30 to 36 (about) fresh raspberries

Raspberry Sauce and Assembly
2 (12-ounce) packages frozen
    raspberries, thawed
½ cup sugar
1 teaspoon lemon juice
2 pints raspberry sorbet
Fresh berries (optional)
Sprigs of mint (optional)

*T*his recipe requires 1 hour of refrigeration and 3 hours freezer time. Preheat the oven to 350 degrees.

For the dough, combine the eggs with enough cold water to generously cover in a saucepan. Bring to a boil over high heat. Boil for 10 minutes; drain. Rinse the eggs with cold water until cool. Peel the eggs and separate, reserving the whites for another recipe. Combine the egg yolks, confectioners' sugar and butter in a mixing bowl. Split the vanilla bean and scrape the seeds into the egg yolk mixture, discarding the pod. Beat with a mixer fitted with a paddle attachment at low speed until creamy. Add the baking powder and flour and mix just until incorporated. Wrap the dough in plastic wrap and chill for 1 hour. Knead the dough on a lightly floured surface to even out the temperature. Roll ¼-inch thick and cut into rounds using a 3¼-inch pastry cutter. Arrange the rounds on a baking sheet. Bake for 10 minutes or until light golden brown. Remove to a wire rack to cool.

For the filling, melt the chocolate in a double boiler over hot water. Scald the cream in a saucepan. Remove the chocolate from the water and add the cream, stirring in a circular motion until blended. Arrange six 2¾-inch flan rings evenly spaced on a baking sheet lined with waxed paper. Place five or six raspberries in each ring. Pour the chocolate mixture over the raspberries, filling the rings to the top. Freeze for 3 hours.

For the sauce, combine the raspberries, sugar and lemon juice in a saucepan. Bring to a low boil over medium-high heat, stirring frequently. Cook for 5 minutes or until the raspberries break down, stirring frequently. Strain through a fine mesh sieve into a bowl, discarding the seeds. Chill, covered, in the refrigerator.

To serve, heat the sides of the flan rings with a kitchen torch to release the chocolate discs; be careful not to overheat the rings or the chocolate will melt. Spoon the sauce in a circle on each of six dessert plates. Place one short dough round in the center of each plate and layer with one chocolate disc. Top each with a scoop of the sorbet and garnish with fresh berries and sprigs of mint. Serves 6.

Photograph for this recipe on page 197.

Grapefruit Granita

1 cup water
1/2 cup superfine sugar
2 cinnamon sticks

2¹/2 cups fresh grapefruit juice
2 teaspoons fresh lemon juice
Sprigs of mint (optional)

*T*his recipe requires 3 hours freezer time. Bring the water and sugar to a boil in a saucepan and add the cinnamon sticks. Boil until the sugar dissolves. Cool for 5 minutes and then discard the cinnamon sticks. Whisk in the grapefruit juice and lemon juice.

Pour into a 9×13-inch freezer dish. Freeze for 3 to 4 hours, scraping with a fork every 30 minutes to break up the ice crystals, especially along the sides of the dish. To serve, scrape the granita with a fork to create a soft crushed ice texture. Spoon into martini glasses and garnish with a sprig of mint. Serve immediately. Serves 4 to 6.

Photograph for this recipe on facing page.

Photograph for this recipe on facing page.

Strawberry Red Wine Sorbet

1 pound strawberries, cut into
   halves or quarters
1 cup sugar
1/2 cup dry red wine

1 vanilla bean, split lengthwise
   into halves
Juice of 1 lemon

*T*his recipe requires 12 hours freezer time. Combine the strawberries, sugar and wine in a bowl and mix well. Scrape the vanilla bean seeds into the strawberry mixture. Add the vanilla bean pod and lemon juice and mix well. Let stand for 45 minutes. Discard the vanilla pod.

Process the strawberry mixture in a blender until puréed. Pour the purée into an ice cream freezer container. Freeze using the manufacturer's directions. Serve immediately. You may store in the freezer for future use. Allow the sorbet to soften slightly before serving. Serves 4.

Grapefruit

The most delicious of the world's grapefruit varieties is the Texas Red grapefruit. This tropical fruit is nurtured in the Rio Grande Valley, where soil and climate allows citrus to attain the highest possible quality. The original red grapefruit was found in the Valley more than seventy years ago growing on a pink grapefruit tree. Named the Ruby Red, this naturally sweet discovery earned Texas the reputation of raising the world's finest grapefruit. Today Texas produces two trademarked categories of red grapefruit, the Ruby Sweet and the Rio Star. Both have red interiors and a rosy blush on the peel. Texas Red grapefruit was named one of Saveur magazine's Top 100 Favorites for 2002.

Butter Pecan Ice Cream

1 cup chopped pecans
1 cup granulated sugar
2 tablespoons butter
2 cups packed light brown sugar

4 cups milk
1 teaspoon vanilla extract
4 cups heavy whipping cream

*T*his recipe requires 2 hours freezer time. Combine the pecans, granulated sugar and butter in a skillet. Cook over medium heat for 6 to 8 minutes or until the sugar dissolves, stirring constantly. Mound the pecan mixture in clusters on a sheet of foil. Let stand until cool. Break the clusters into small chunks.

Combine the brown sugar, milk and vanilla in a bowl and stir until the brown sugar dissolves. Stir in the pecan chunks and the cream. Pour into an ice cream freezer container. Freeze using the manufacturer's directions. Remove the ice cream to a freezer-safe container and freeze, covered, for 2 hours before serving. This recipe may be cut in half. Serves 6 to 9.

Almond Brittle

1 cup (2 sticks) butter
1 cup sugar

2 tablespoons light corn syrup
2 cups sliced almonds

*C*oat the shiny side of an 18×30-inch piece of foil with butter. Melt 1 cup butter in a saucepan and stir in the sugar, corn syrup and almonds in the order listed. Cook over medium-low heat until the mixture reaches 300 to 310 degrees on a candy thermometer or is a deep caramel color, stirring constantly. Pour onto the prepared foil and press with the bottom of a buttered glass pie plate until the mixture is as thin as possible. Let stand until cool. Peel off the foil and break the brittle into bite-size pieces. Store in an airtight container. Serves 8 to 12.

Photograph for this recipe on page 224.

Caramel Corn

3 cups packed brown sugar
1 cup light corn syrup
1 cup (2 sticks) butter
1/2 cup water

2 teaspoons cream of tartar
1/2 teaspoon baking soda
4 cups popcorn, popped

Combine the brown sugar, corn syrup, butter, water and cream of tartar in a saucepan. Cook to 140 degrees on a candy thermometer, soft-ball stage. Remove from the heat and whisk in the baking soda until the mixture is light in color. Toss with the popcorn in a bowl until coated. Serves 6 to 8.

Peanut Butter Bon Bons

1 1/3 cups peanut butter
1 cup (2 sticks) margarine
2 teaspoons vanilla extract
4 cups confectioners' sugar

1/4 block paraffin
2 cups (12 ounces) milk
    chocolate chips

What Is Cream of Tartar?

Cream of tartar gives volume to egg whites and helps stabilize them when whipped in to a meringue. The white powder is derived from tartaric acid, the white crystals that form during the wine making fermentation process with grapes.

This recipe requires 4 hours of refrigeration. Beat the peanut butter, margarine and vanilla in a mixing bowl until blended. Add the confectioners' sugar gradually, beating constantly until thick and creamy. Shape the peanut butter mixture into 1 1/2-inch balls. Arrange the balls on a baking sheet and chill for 2 hours or until very firm.

Melt the paraffin in a double boiler over medium heat. Add the chocolate chips and cook until melted and creamy, stirring occasionally. Decrease the heat to low to prevent the chocolate from becoming grainy.

Drop the peanut butter balls one at a time into the chocolate. Remove by scooping the balls with the tines of a fork and slowly allowing the balls to slide off onto a tray lined with waxed paper. Chill for 2 hours or until set. This will ensure the bon bons have a glossy finish. Store in an airtight container in the refrigerator for up to 1 month. Makes 5 dozen bon bons.

Photograph for this recipe on page 197.

Perfect Fudge

2 1/2 cups sugar
1/2 cup light corn syrup

1/2 cup milk
1/2 cup (1 stick) margarine
2 ounces unsweetened chocolate

1 cup chopped pecans
1 teaspoon vanilla extract

This recipe requires refrigeration time. Bring the sugar, corn syrup, milk, margarine and chocolate to a rolling boil in a saucepan. Boil for 3 minutes, stirring constantly. Remove from the heat and stir in the pecans and vanilla. Beat with a mixer for 12 to 15 minutes or until the mixtures starts to loose its luster. Spread in a buttered 2-quart dish.

Let stand at room temperature until completely cooled. This will prevent crystallization on the top. Place the fudge in the refrigerator. Cut into squares and serve. This recipe works best when the humidity is low. Makes 2 dozen squares.

Autumn Apple Cake

1 cup vegetable oil
2 cups granulated sugar
3 eggs
2 1/2 cups all-purpose flour
1 1/2 teaspoons baking soda

1/2 teaspoon salt
1/4 teaspoon ground cloves
1/4 teaspoon nutmeg
2 teaspoons cinnamon
2 teaspoons vanilla extract

3 cups grated apples
   (about 3 large apples)
1 cup chopped pecans
1 cup confectioners' sugar
Milk

Preheat the oven to 350 degrees. Combine the oil, granulated sugar, eggs, flour, baking soda, salt, cloves, nutmeg, cinnamon and vanilla in a bowl in the order listed and mix well. Stir in the apples and pecans. Spoon the batter into a greased and floured bundt pan. Bake for 1 hour or until a wooden pick inserted near the center comes out clean. Cool in the pan on a wire rack for 10 minutes. Invert onto a cake plate and cool slightly.

Pour the confectioners' sugar into a bowl. Add enough milk 1 teaspoon at a time until of a glaze consistency, stirring constantly. Pour over the top of the warm cake, allowing the glaze to drizzle down the side. Serves 12.

Carrot Cake

Cake

2 cups plus 2 tablespoons
    cake flour
2 teaspoons baking soda
2 teaspoons cinnamon
1/2 teaspoon salt
1 cup chopped pecans
4 eggs
1 1/2 cups vegetable oil
2 cups sugar
3 cups packed shredded carrots
    (about 2 pounds)

Cream Cheese Frosting

12 ounces cream cheese, softened
3/4 cup (1 1/2 sticks) unsalted
    butter, softened
1/4 teaspoon salt
3 cups confectioners' sugar
2 teaspoons vanilla extract

*P*reheat the oven to 350 degrees.

For the cake, combine the cake flour, baking soda, cinnamon and salt in a bowl and mix with a fork to aerate. Stir in the pecans. Beat the eggs in a mixing bowl for 5 minutes or until pale yellow and fluffy. Beat in the oil. Add the sugar gradually, beating constantly until blended. Fold in the flour mixture and carrots. Spoon the batter into three greased and floured 8-inch cake pans or two greased and floured 9-inch cake pans. Bake for 30 minutes or until the layers test done. Cool in the pans for 10 minutes. Remove to a wire rack to cool completely.

For the frosting, beat the cream cheese and butter in a mixing bowl until creamy. Blend in the salt. Add the confectioners' sugar gradually, beating constantly until of a spreading consistency. Stir in the vanilla. Spread the frosting between the layers and over the top and side of the cake. Serves 12.

Carrots

Texas ranks fifth in U.S. carrot production, with annual revenues exceeding $20 million. Some 60 percent is grown for the fresh market with the remainder going for processing. Beta Sweet, a maroon carrot developed at Texas A&M University, shows sales potential among health-conscious consumers. Beta Sweets contain about 40 percent more beta carotene, as well as more anthocyanin, than typical orange carrots. These antioxidants may help prevent cancer.

Decadent Chocolate Cake with Whipped Frosting

Cake

1³/4 cups all-purpose flour, sifted

2 cups sugar

³/4 cup baking cocoa

1¹/2 teaspoons baking powder

1¹/2 teaspoons baking soda

1 teaspoon salt

1 cup milk (do not use skim milk)

¹/2 cup canola oil

2 eggs

2 tablespoons anisette

2 teaspoons vanilla extract

1 cup boiling water

Whipped Frosting

1¹/2 cups heavy whipping cream, chilled

1¹/2 teaspoons confectioners' sugar

¹/4 cup plus 2 tablespoons granulated sugar

1¹/2 tablespoons baking cocoa

Chocolate curls (optional)

Preheat the oven to 350 degrees.

For the cake, coat the bottoms of two 9-inch cake pans with butter. Line the bottoms with baking parchment and brush the parchment paper and sides of the pans with butter. Dust with flour.

Mix 1³/4 cups flour, the sugar, baking cocoa, baking powder, baking soda and salt in a large mixing bowl. Add the milk, canola oil, eggs, liqueur and vanilla and beat at medium speed for 2 minutes. Reduce the speed to low and beat in the boiling water until blended.

Pour the batter evenly into the prepared pans. Bake for 30 to 35 minutes or until a wooden skewer inserted in the middle of each layer comes out clean. Cool in the pans on a wire rack for 10 minutes. Invert onto the wire rack to cool completely.

For the frosting, beat the cream and confectioners' sugar in a mixing bowl until soft peaks form. Gently fold in the granulated sugar and baking cocoa. Arrange one of the cake layers on a cake plate. Spread with one-third of the frosting. Top with the remaining cake layer and spread the remaining frosting over the side and top of the cake. Garnish with chocolate curls. Serve immediately or store, covered, in the refrigerator.

For a different presentation, spread most of the frosting between the layers. Dust the top with additional baking cocoa and garnish each serving with a dollop of the remaining frosting and a chocolate curl. Serves 16.

Photograph for this recipe on facing page and on page 196.

Chocolate Texas Sheet Cake

Cake
2 cups sugar
2 cups all-purpose flour
1 teaspoon baking soda
1/2 cup buttermilk
2 eggs

1 teaspoon cinnamon
1 teaspoon vanilla extract
1 cup water
1/2 cup (1 stick) margarine
1/2 cup vegetable oil
1/4 cup baking cocoa

Chocolate Icing
1/2 cup (1 stick) margarine
6 tablespoons milk
1/4 cup baking cocoa
Pinch of salt
2 cups confectioners' sugar

This recipe requires refrigeration time. Preheat the oven to 400 degrees.

For the cake, mix the sugar, flour and baking soda in a mixing bowl. Add the buttermilk, eggs, cinnamon and vanilla and beat until blended. Bring the water, margarine, oil and baking cocoa to a boil in a small saucepan. Add to the buttermilk mixture and stir until blended.

Pour the batter into a greased 9×13-inch cake pan. Bake for 18 to 22 minutes or until the edges pull from the sides of the pan. Cool for 15 minutes before icing.

For the icing, bring the margarine, milk, baking cocoa and salt to a boil in a saucepan, stirring constantly. Pour over the confectioners' sugar in a bowl and stir until blended. Pour the icing evenly over the top of the warm cake. Chill, covered, in the refrigerator until set. Serves 12 to 15.

Substitution for Buttermilk

Out of buttermilk? In a small bowl or glass, add one tablespoon of lemon juice to one cup of milk. Allow to rest for 3 minutes before use. Be sure to measure the appropriate amount of liquid before adding it to your recipe.

The first event at our dining room table was my sister's baby shower a couple of years ago. I covered the table in pink rose petals, pastel butterflies, and painted ceramic Easter eggs since the shower was so close to Easter—babies and eggs just seem to go together. In the middle of the table was a homemade pink strawberry cake waiting for us to share. The table is a dark mahogany color with a light green glass inlay in the middle. The contrast of the strong, straight-lined table with the softness of the things on it seemed so picturesque. It was one of the first times I felt all grown up. It is funny how something like owning a dining room table can make you feel grown up.   —V. Sudderth

"That's So Italian" Cream Cake

Cake
2 cups all-purpose flour
1 teaspoon baking soda
2 cups sugar
1/2 cup (1 stick) margarine
1/2 cup shortening
5 egg yolks
1 cup buttermilk
1 1/2 teaspoons vanilla extract

5 egg whites
1 (3-ounce) can shredded coconut
1 cup chopped pecans

**Cream Cheese Icing
and Assembly**
1/2 cup (1 stick)
    margarine, softened
16 ounces cream cheese, softened

3 cups confectioners' sugar
2 teaspoons vanilla extract
1 1/2 cups chopped pecans

Preheat the oven to 350 degrees.

For the cake, mix the flour and baking soda together. Beat the sugar, margarine and shortening in a mixing bowl until creamy. Add the egg yolks and beat until blended. Add the flour mixture and buttermilk alternately, beating well after each addition. Blend in the vanilla. Beat the egg whites in a mixing bowl until peaks form and fold into the batter.

Pour the batter evenly into three greased 8-inch cake pans. Bake for 25 minutes or until the layers test done. Cool in the pans for 10 minutes. Remove to a wire rack to cool completely.

For the icing, combine the margarine, cream cheese, confectioners' sugar and vanilla in a mixing bowl and beat until of a spreading consistency. Fold in the pecans. Spread the icing between the layers and over the top and side of the cake. Store, covered, in the refrigerator. Serves 12 to 14.

Birthday Cakes

The history of birthday cakes can be traced back to two primary cultures— the ancient Greeks and the Germans of the Middle Ages. In ancient Greece, cakes in the shape of the moon (hence, cakes being round) were delivered to the goddess of the moon, Artemis. Candles were placed on the cake to create a glow like the moon. During the Middle Ages, it was popular to make a cake to celebrate the birth of Jesus, a tradition which evolved into Kinderfest cakes, cakes made to celebrate any youth's day of birth.

Pumpkin Praline Cake

Cake

2 cups all-purpose flour
2 teaspoons baking powder
2 teaspoons pumpkin pie spice
1 teaspoon baking soda
1 teaspoon salt
3/4 cup packed brown sugar
1/3 cup butter

3 tablespoons whipping cream
3/4 cup chopped pecans
1 2/3 cups granulated sugar
1 cup vegetable oil
4 eggs
2 cups cooked fresh or
    canned pumpkin
1/4 teaspoon vanilla extract

Whipped Cream Topping and Assembly

1 3/4 cups heavy whipping cream
1/4 cup confectioners' sugar
1/4 teaspoon vanilla extract
Chopped pecans (optional)

*P*reheat the oven to 350 degrees.

For the cake, mix the flour, baking powder, pumpkin pie spice, baking soda and salt in a bowl. Combine the brown sugar, butter and cream in a saucepan. Cook over low heat until the brown sugar dissolves, stirring constantly. Pour evenly into two greased 9-inch springform pans. Sprinkle with the pecans. Let stand until cool.

Beat the granulated sugar, oil and eggs in a mixing bowl until blended. Add the pumpkin and vanilla and beat until smooth. Add the dry ingredients and beat just until blended. Spoon the pumpkin mixture evenly over the prepared layers. Bake for 30 to 35 minutes or until a wooden pick inserted near the center comes out clean. Cool in the pans for 5 minutes. Remove to a wire rack to cool completely.

For the topping, beat the cream in a mixing bowl until soft peaks form. Add the confectioners' sugar and vanilla and beat until blended. Place one cake layer praline side up on a cake plate and spread with two-thirds of the topping. Top with the remaining cake layer praline side up and spread with the remaining topping. Sprinkle with pecans. Store, covered, in the refrigerator. For variety, spread all the topping between the layers and sprinkle with pecans. Cut the recipe in half for a one-layer cake. Serves 14.

Photograph for this recipe on facing page.

Baking Powder and Baking Soda

Leavening in baking is the purpose of both baking powder and baking soda. How does this happen? Your baked goods rise because both of these substances produce carbon dioxide which aerates your dough or batter, or causes it to "rise." An acid is necessary to cause this reaction with both; baking soda is added to recipes that contain an acid such as yogurt or buttermilk. Baking powder contains both the base (baking soda) and an acid (usually cream of tartar). Out of baking powder? Make your own— combine one part baking soda with two parts cream of tartar.

Layered Lemon Curd Cake

Cake

1 cup plain yogurt
1 teaspoon baking soda
6 tablespoons fresh lemon juice
6 tablespoons orange juice
2 cups bread flour
1 tablespoon baking powder
1/2 teaspoon salt
1 cup (2 sticks) unsalted
  butter, softened
1 cup sugar
1 1/2 tablespoons chopped
  lemon zest
4 eggs, at room temperature

**Lemon Cream Cheese Frosting
and Assembly**

8 ounces cream cheese, softened
1/2 cup (1 stick) unsalted
  butter, softened
8 cups confectioners' sugar
2 to 3 tablespoons lemon curd
1 (12-ounce) jar lemon curd,
  heated in the microwave
1 1/2 tablespoons chopped lemon
  zest (optional)
1 ounce pistachios or almonds,
  toasted and chopped (optional)

*T*his recipe requires 2 hours of refrigeration. Preheat the oven to 350 degrees.

For the cake, line the bottoms of three 6-inch springform pans or cake pans with waxed paper or baking parchment and spray with nonstick cooking spray. Combine the yogurt and baking soda in a bowl and mix well. Let stand for 10 minutes. Stir in the lemon juice and orange juice.

Mix the bread flour, baking powder and salt together. Combine the butter, sugar and lemon zest in a mixing bowl and beat until combined. Add the eggs one at a time, beating well after each addition. Add the yogurt mixture and dry ingredients alternately, beating well after each addition. Divide the batter evenly among the prepared pans. Bake for 12 to 15 minutes or until firm to the touch. Invert onto a wire rack to cool.

For the frosting, beat the cream cheese and butter in a mixing bowl until creamy. Add the confectioners' sugar 1 cup at a time, beating after each addition. Blend in 2 to 3 tablespoons lemon curd.

Place one cake layer upside down on a cake plate or platter. Spread half the warm lemon curd over the layer. Top with a second cake layer and spread with the remaining warm lemon curd. Top with the remaining cake layer. Spread the side and top of the cake with the frosting. Sprinkle with the lemon zest. Gently press the pistachios around the bottom 1 inch of the cake. Chill, covered, for at least 2 hours or until ready to serve. Serves 12 to 15.

Photograph for this recipe on page 196.

Yum Yum Cake

2 cups all-purpose flour
2 cups sugar
2 teaspoons baking soda
1/2 teaspoon salt

2 eggs, beaten
1 (20-ounce) can crushed pineapple
1/2 cup (1 stick) butter
1 (5-ounce) can evaporated milk

1 cup sugar
1 cup shredded coconut
1 cup pecans
1 teaspoon vanilla extract

*P*reheat the oven to 350 degrees. Mix the flour, 2 cups sugar, baking soda and salt in a bowl. Stir in the eggs and undrained pineapple. Spread in a 9×12-inch cake pan. Bake for 30 minutes. Combine the butter, evaporated milk and 1 cup sugar in a saucepan. Boil for 2 minutes. Stir in the coconut, pecans and vanilla. Pierce the cake all over with a fork. Pour over the hot cake. Serves 12 to 14.

Cinnamon-Dusted Chocolate Cupcakes

Cupcakes
2²/3 cups all-purpose flour
1¹/2 cups baking cocoa
1 tablespoon cinnamon
1¹/2 teaspoons baking powder
1 teaspoon baking soda
1 teaspoon salt
3¹/2 cups sugar

2 eggs
2 egg yolks
1¹/4 cups buttermilk
3/4 cup vegetable oil
1/4 cup coffee, cooled
1 tablespoon vanilla extract
1 cup (6 ounces) semisweet
    chocolate chips

Cream Cheese Frosting
6 ounces cream cheese, softened
1 (1-pound) package
    confectioners' sugar
1 to 2 tablespoons milk
1/2 to 3/4 teaspoon good-quality
    almond extract

*P*reheat the oven to 325 degrees.

For the cupcakes, mix the flour, baking cocoa, cinnamon, baking powder, baking soda and salt together. Beat the sugar, eggs and egg yolks in a mixing bowl until blended. Add the buttermilk, oil, coffee and vanilla gradually and beat until smooth. Add the dry ingredients and beat at medium speed just until blended. Stir in the chocolate chips. Pour into paper-lined muffin cups. Bake for 20 to 25 minutes or until a wooden pick inserted near the center comes out clean. Cool in the pan for 2 minutes. Remove to a wire rack to cool completely.

For the frosting, beat the cream cheese in a mixing bowl for about 2 minutes. Gradually add the confectioners' sugar, beating constantly until blended. Add the milk and flavoring and beat at high speed for 2 minutes or until smooth, adding additional milk if needed for the desired consistency. Spread over the cupcakes. Store, covered, in the refrigerator. Bring to room temperature before serving. Makes 30 cupcakes.

Chocolate Chip Bars

2 cups all-purpose flour
1 teaspoon baking powder
1/2 teaspoon salt

1/4 teaspoon baking soda
2/3 cup margarine, softened
2 cups packed brown sugar
2 eggs

2 teaspoons vanilla extract
2 cups (12 ounces) semisweet
   chocolate chips
2 cups pecans, chopped

*P*reheat the oven to 350 degrees. Sift the flour, baking powder, salt and baking soda together. Beat the margarine in a mixing bowl until creamy. Add the brown sugar gradually, beating constantly until fluffy. Beat in the eggs and vanilla until blended. Mix in the dry ingredients. Fold in the chocolate chips and pecans. Spread the batter in a greased 9×13-inch baking pan. Bake for 25 minutes. Cool in the pan on a wire rack. Cut into bars. Store in an airtight container. Makes 2 to 3 dozen bars.

Photograph for this recipe on page 224.

Mississippi Mud Brownies

1 cup (2 sticks) margarine, melted
   and cooled
1/2 cup baking cocoa
2 cups granulated sugar
4 eggs, lightly beaten

1 1/2 cups all-purpose flour
1 1/2 teaspoons salt
1 teaspoon vanilla extract
1 to 2 cups pecans or walnuts
1 (16-ounce) package miniature
   marshmallows

2 cups confectioners' sugar
1/2 cup (1 stick) margarine,
   softened
6 tablespoons evaporated milk
6 tablespoons baking cocoa
1 teaspoon vanilla extract

*P*reheat the oven to 350 degrees. Combine 1 cup margarine and 1/2 cup baking cocoa in a bowl and mix well. Stir in the granulated sugar, eggs and flour in the order listed, mixing until blended after each addition. Add the salt, vanilla and pecans and mix well. Spread the batter in a greased 9×13-inch baking pan. Bake for 25 to 28 minutes or until the brownies pull from the edges of the pan. Remove from the oven and immediately sprinkle with the marshmallows. Bake for 3 to 4 minutes or just until the marshmallows begin to melt; watch carefully. Cool in the pan on a wire rack. Mix the confectioners' sugar, 1/2 cup margarine, the evaporated milk, 6 tablespoons baking cocoa and the vanilla in a bowl until of a spreading consistency. Spread the icing over the baked layers. Chill for 1 hour before cutting into bars for a neater cut. Serve at room temperature. Store in an airtight container at room temperature. Makes 2 dozen brownies.

Peppermint Squares

20 graham crackers, crushed
1 cup (2 sticks) butter, softened
1/2 cup finely chopped walnuts
1 1/2 cups confectioners' sugar
3 eggs

12 ounces milk chocolate or
    dark chocolate candy bar or
    bark, melted
2 cups heavy whipping cream
1/2 cup ground peppermint candy

1 cup chopped walnuts
Coarsely ground
    peppermint candy

This recipe requires 24 hours freezer time. Mix the graham cracker crumbs, 1/2 cup of the butter and 1/2 cup walnuts in a bowl. Press over the bottom of a 9×13-inch dish, or use a smaller dish for a thicker crust. Beat the confectioners' sugar with the remaining 1/2 cup butter in a mixing bowl until creamy. Add the eggs and beat until blended. Mix in the melted chocolate and pour over the prepared layer. Beat the cream in a mixing bowl until soft peaks form. Fold in 1/2 cup ground peppermint and 1 cup walnuts. Spread over the prepared layers. Sprinkle with coarsely ground peppermint. Freeze, covered, for 24 hours. Cut into squares and place in an airtight container. Freeze until serving time. Remove from the freezer a few minutes before serving. Substitute whipped topping for the whipped cream, if desired. Makes 1 dozen squares.

> *If you are concerned about using raw eggs, use eggs pasteurized in their shells, which are sold at some specialty food stores, or use an equivalent amount of pasteurized egg substitute.*

Chocolate Crinkles

2 cups sifted all-purpose flour
2 teaspoons baking powder
1/2 teaspoon salt
1 2/3 cups granulated sugar
1/2 cup shortening

2 teaspoons vanilla extract
2 eggs
2 ounces unsweetened
    chocolate, melted
1/3 cup milk

1/2 cup chopped walnuts (optional)
Sifted confectioners' sugar

This recipe requires 3 hours of refrigeration. Preheat the oven to 350 degrees. Sift the flour, baking powder and salt together. Beat the granulated sugar, shortening and vanilla in a mixing bowl until creamy. Add the eggs and beat until blended. Mix in the chocolate. Add the dry ingredients and milk alternately, beating well after each addition. Stir in the walnuts. Chill, covered, for 3 hours. Shape the dough into 1-inch balls; coat with confectioners' sugar. Arrange 2 inches apart on a greased cookie sheet. Bake for about 15 minutes. Cool on the cookie sheet for 2 minutes. Remove to a wire rack to cool completely. Store in an airtight container. Makes 2 dozen crinkles.

Photograph for this recipe on page 224.

Roll-out-the-Rugelach

4 ounces cream cheese, chilled and
cut into 4 pieces
1/2 cup (1 stick) unsalted butter,
chilled and cut into 4 pieces
1 cup all-purpose flour
1/4 teaspoon salt
1/2 cup seedless raspberry jam or
apricot jam
2 tablespoons granulated sugar
1/2 teaspoon cinnamon

1/4 cup chopped walnuts, almonds
or pecans
1/4 cup currants, plumped
(optional)
4 ounces bittersweet chocolate or
milk chocolate, finely chopped
1 egg
1 teaspoon cream
2 tablespoons coarse
decorating sugar

This recipe requires 4 1/2 hours of refrigeration. Position the oven racks to divide the oven into thirds. Preheat the oven to 350 degrees. Let the cream cheese and butter stand at room temperature for 10 minutes or until softened but still cool. Pulse the cream cheese, butter, flour and salt in a food processor six to ten times or just until the dough forms large curds, scraping the side of the bowl frequently. Do not process long enough for the dough to form a ball. Shape the dough into a ball and divide into two equal portions. Shape each portion into a disc and wrap in plastic wrap. Chill for 4 to 8 hours.

Heat the jam in a saucepan over low heat until melted. Mix the granulated sugar and cinnamon in a small bowl. Roll each dough disc into a 9- to 10-inch round on a lightly floured surface. Let the dough stand at room temperature for 10 minutes or pound with a rolling pin a few times if too firm to roll.

Brush a thin layer of the jam over each round and sprinkle each with half the sugar and cinnamon mixture, half the walnuts, half the currants and half the chocolate. Gently press the filling into the rounds using a sheet of waxed paper. Discard the waxed paper. Cut each round into fourteen wedges or triangles. Roll each wedge into a crescent. Arrange the crescents on a cookie sheet lined with baking parchment or a silicone mat, making sure the points are tucked under. Chill for 30 minutes or longer.

Whisk the egg and cream in a small bowl until blended. Brush the crescents with the egg mixture and sprinkle with the decorating sugar. Bake for 20 to 25 minutes or until puffed and golden brown, rotating the cookie sheets from top to bottom and front to back halfway through the baking process. Cool on the cookie sheet for 2 minutes. Remove to a wire rack to cool completely. Store in an airtight container. Makes 28 cookies.

Photograph for this recipe on facing page.

Toffee Crunch Cookies

1³/4 cups all-purpose flour
1 teaspoon salt
1/2 teaspoon baking soda
1/2 cup butter-flavor shortening

1/2 cup (1 stick) butter
1 cup granulated sugar
1 cup packed brown sugar
1 (14-ounce) can sweetened
    condensed milk

1 teaspoon vanilla extract
3 cups quick-cooking oats
1 to 2 cups toffee pieces
1 cup (6 ounces) milk
    chocolate chips

You may add nuts of your choice to the batter or substitute chopped nuts for the toffee pieces.

Preheat the oven to 350 degrees. Mix the flour, salt and baking soda together. Combine the shortening, butter, granulated sugar and brown sugar in a large bowl and stir with a spoon until blended and creamy. Add the condensed milk and vanilla and mix well. Blend in the flour mixture and stir in the oats. Shape the dough into 1-inch balls. Press the tops of the balls into the toffee pieces. Arrange the balls toffee side up 2 inches apart on a cookie sheet sprayed with nonstick cooking spray. Bake for 9 to 10 minutes or until set but not brown. Cool for 2 minutes and remove to a wire rack to cool completely.

Place the chocolate chips in a heavy sealable plastic bag and seal tightly. Microwave on Medium for 1 minute; knead the bag. Repeat the process until the chocolate chips are melted and smooth. Cut a tiny tip off the corner of the bag and drizzle the chocolate over the cooled cookies. Let stand until set. Store in an airtight container. Makes 2 dozen cookies.

Peanut Butter Cookies

2 cups sifted all-purpose flour
2 teaspoons baking soda
1/2 teaspoon salt

1 cup shortening
1 cup granulated sugar
1 cup packed brown sugar

1 cup peanut butter
2 eggs
1 teaspoon vanilla extract

Preheat the oven to 350 degrees. Mix the flour, baking soda and salt together. Beat the shortening, granulated sugar, brown sugar, peanut butter, eggs and vanilla in a mixing bowl until creamy. Add the flour mixture gradually and beat just until combined. Shape the peanut butter mixture into balls and arrange on a cookie sheet. Flatten the balls with a fork, making a crisscross pattern. Bake for 8 minutes. Cool on the cookie sheet for 2 minutes. Cool on a wire rack. Store in an airtight container. Makes 2 dozen cookies.

Photograph for these recipes on page 224.

Tea Cake Sugar Cookies

4 cups all-purpose flour
2 cups granulated sugar
1 1/2 teaspoons baking powder
1 teaspoon salt
1 cup (2 sticks) margarine

1 cup buttermilk
2 eggs
1 1/2 to 2 teaspoons vanilla extract
1 teaspoon baking soda
1/4 cup (1/2 stick) margarine

3 tablespoons evaporated milk
1 teaspoon vanilla extract
2 cups confectioners' sugar
Food coloring (optional)

Preheat the oven to 375 degrees. Sift the flour, granulated sugar, baking powder and salt into a bowl and mix well. Cut 1 cup margarine into the flour mixture. Make a well in the center of the flour mixture. Whisk the buttermilk, eggs, 1 1/2 to 2 teaspoons vanilla and the baking soda in a bowl until blended. Add the buttermilk mixture to the well and stir with a spoon just until combined; do not overmix.

Roll the dough 1/4 inch thick on a lightly floured surface, adding additional flour as needed for rolling. Cut into the desired shapes. Arrange on a cookie sheet and bake for 8 to 10 minutes or until light brown. Cool on the cookie sheet for 2 minutes. Remove to a wire rack to cool completely.

Beat 1/4 cup margarine, the evaporated milk and 1 teaspoon vanilla in a mixing bowl until creamy. Add the confectioners' sugar and beat until of a spreading consistency, adding additional milk and/or additional confectioners' sugar as needed for the desired consistency. Stir in food coloring. Spread the icing over the cooled cookies. Let stand until set. Serve for dessert or with coffee for breakfast. Make for Easter or Christmas using holiday cookie cutters. Makes 2 dozen cookies.

Photograph for this recipe on page 224.

As a teacher, I had the week before Christmas off. This made me the perfect candidate to babysit my niece and nephew along with my own three children! I always tried to think up fun activities to keep them occupied during this exciting time. One of their favorites was decorating their very own gingerbread houses. I would put the houses together ahead of time using graham crackers and royal icing, that magic icing that dries as hard as a rock, so the houses could withstand "preschool force." Then the kids would "go to town" decorating with gumdrops, candy pieces, and additional icing and sprinkles. The table and floor were covered; little sprinkles would show up in the strangest places for months! Despite the mess, the children had a fun time, and they were so proud of their gingerbread houses that they had made "all by themselves." —J. Price

Rich and Creamy Chocolate Pie

Refrigerator pie pastry dough
1 1/2 cups sugar
1/3 cup plus 1 tablespoon
   all-purpose flour
5 tablespoons baking cocoa

1/8 teaspoon salt
3 cups milk
3 egg yolks, lightly beaten
1 tablespoon butter
1 1/2 teaspoons vanilla extract

8 egg whites, at room temperature
1/2 teaspoon cream of tartar
2 pinches of salt
1 cup sugar

Roll the pie pastry on a lightly floured surface from the center to the edge until the dough is 1/4 inch thick. Fit the pastry into a 9-inch pie plate and trim 1/2 to 1 inch beyond the edge. Fold the pastry under and flute the edge. Prick the bottom and side with a fork. Bake using the package directions for 10 minutes or until golden brown. Let stand until cool.

Combine 1 1/2 cups sugar, the flour, baking cocoa and 1/8 teaspoon salt in a bowl. Whisk the milk and egg yolks in a saucepan until blended. Add the sugar mixture and mix well. Bring to a boil over medium heat and boil until thickened, stirring constantly. The filling should be very thick. Remove from the heat and stir in the butter and vanilla. Spread in the baked pie shell.

Place the oven rack in the highest position. Change the oven to the broiler setting. Beat the egg whites, cream of tartar and 2 pinches of salt in a mixing bowl with an electric mixer until soft peaks form. Add 1 cup sugar gradually, beating constantly until stiff, glossy peaks form; do not overbeat. Spread the meringue over the warm filling using a rubber spatula, sealing to the edge. Make decorative peaks in the meringue using the back of a spoon. Broil for 1 to 2 minutes or until golden brown and set, watching carefully to prevent overbrowning. Cool on a wire rack before serving. Serves 10.

Sometimes a pie is much more than just a sweet end to a meal. For my family, it is this chocolate pie. Passed down through generations, this pie brings back fond memories and is always a special treat. In our family, it's called "Un's Chocolate Pie." "Un" is what my younger brothers started calling our grandmother before they were a year old because they could not pronounce her name, Evelyn. She made this pie for her two sons and now makes it for her two grandsons. This is their pie; she won't make it for anyone else and never has.

My mother got the recipe several years ago but has never made it. When the Texas Tables project started, I thought "Un's Chocolate Pie" would be a great addition. Evelyn Young is now eighty-nine years old and is still making her chocolate pies for my brothers, who are now in their twenties. If I'm lucky, I occasionally get a piece of Un's famous pie when I stop by for a visit.
—A. Boudreaux

Amazing Coconut Cream Pie

3 cups flaked coconut
1 1/2 tablespoons butter
3 cups half-and-half
3/4 cup sugar

1/2 cup all-purpose flour
2 eggs, lightly beaten
1/4 teaspoon salt
3/4 cup flaked coconut, toasted

1 teaspoon vanilla extract
2 cups heavy whipping cream
3 tablespoons sugar
1/4 cup flaked coconut, toasted

*T*his recipe requires 2 hours of refrigeration. Preheat the oven to 325 degrees. Mix 3 cups coconut and the butter in a bowl until combined. Press the coconut mixture over the bottom and up the side of an 8- or 9-inch pie plate. Bake for 15 minutes.

Combine the half-and-half, 3/4 cup sugar, the flour, eggs and salt in a medium saucepan and mix well. Bring to a boil over low heat, stirring constantly. Remove from the heat and stir in 3/4 cup toasted coconut and the vanilla. Pour into the baked crust. Chill for 2 to 4 hours or until set. Beat the cream and 3 tablespoons sugar in a mixing bowl until thickened. Spread the whipped cream over the filling and sprinkle with 1/4 cup toasted coconut. Store in the refrigerator.

To toast coconut, spread the coconut on an ungreased baking sheet. Toast at 350 degrees for 5 to 7 minutes or until golden brown, stirring occasionally. Serves 10.

The Perfect Margarita Pie

1/2 cup (1 stick) butter
1 1/4 cups finely crushed pretzels
1/4 cup sugar
1 (14-ounce) can sweetened
    condensed milk

1/3 cup lime juice
1/4 cup gold tequila
2 tablespoons Triple Sec or any
    orange liqueur

1 cup heavy whipping
    cream, whipped

*T*his recipe requires about 4 hours of refrigeration. Melt the butter in a saucepan and stir in the pretzels and sugar. Press the pretzel mixture over the bottom and up the side of a 9-inch pie plate. Chill in the refrigerator.

Combine the condensed milk, lime juice, tequila and liqueur in a bowl and mix well. Fold in the whipped cream and spread the filling in the prepared crust. Chill for about 4 hours. Garnish as desired. Store in the refrigerator. Serves 10.

The Bar

Cocktails often accompany a celebration, whether we are toasting loved ones for an accomplishment or sharing a, "Cheers!" with friends over a special moment. Libation equally has its place while we share a laugh with an old friend or just relax poolside after a long day of work and activities. The perfectly crafted beverage, served in crystal or plastic, can help make a gathering an event or turn a simple occasion into a celebration. Specialty drinks partner beautifully with our favorite moments, adding a celebratory mood to even the most simple of get-togethers.

"And do as adversaries do in law,
strive mightily, but eat and drink as friends."

—William Shakespeare

Almond Iced Tea

2 cups hot water
1 cup sugar
3 tablespoons instant tea
1 1/2 tablespoons vanilla extract

1 tablespoon almond extract
1 (12-ounce) can frozen lemonade
  concentrate
8 1/2 cups cold water

*T*his recipe requires refrigeration. Combine the hot water, sugar and instant tea in a large heatproof pitcher and mix until the sugar and tea dissolve. Stir in the flavorings and lemonade concentrate. Add the cold water and mix well. Chill in the refrigerator. Pour over ice in glasses. Serves 4 to 6.

Miss Priss Punch

1 (32-ounce) bottle cranberry juice
1 (16-ounce) can orange juice
1 (6-ounce) can pineapple juice
2 oranges, sliced
1 lemon, sliced

1 (50-ounce) bottle ginger
  ale, chilled
1 pint raspberries (optional)
1 pint blueberries (optional)
1 bunch fresh mint (optional)

*T*his recipe requires refrigeration. Combine the cranberry juice, orange juice, pineapple juice, oranges and lemon in a large container and mix well. Chill, covered, for several hours. Pour into a punch bowl. Stir in the ginger ale, raspberries and blueberries. Ladle into punch cups and garnish each serving with fresh mint. Great for parties, especially showers. Serves 30.

*M*y grandparents from Fort Worth built me a scallop-edged wooden table with three stools when I was four years old. I loved to have tea parties with my dolls and animals and even sit at my table and read books. My sister enjoyed the same table when she turned four. My daughter now has the table in her room and loves to have tea parties, color, and read at her table. The table has also been used as the "kids table" at Christmas time with cousins. For over thirty-four years, this table has provided a place to be imaginative and creative while establishing lasting memories with family and friends.   —S. Mills

Amaretto Slush

4 cups amaretto
1 (46-ounce) can pineapple juice
18 ounces frozen pink lemonade
  concentrate, thawed

1/3 cup lemon juice
3 liters lemon-lime soda, chilled

This recipe requires 8 hours freezer time. Combine the liqueur, pineapple juice, lemonade concentrate and lemon juice in a large freezer container and mix well. Freeze, covered, for 8 hours or longer, stirring twice.

To serve, combine equal portions of the frozen amaretto mixture and soda in glasses. Serve immediately. Store leftover amaretto mixture in the freezer. You may serve in a punch bowl. Serves 20 to 24.

Iced Brandy Alexander

1 pint vanilla ice cream
2 ounces Kahlúa or other coffee
  liqueur such as Tia Maria

2 1/2 ounces brandy
2 dashes nutmeg (optional)

Process the ice cream, liqueur and brandy in a blender until smooth. Pour into two wine glasses and garnish with the nutmeg. Serve immediately. Serves 2.

We are a family that loves to celebrate everything—and always all together. We've celebrated graduations, births, engagements, weddings, and every holiday. One of the most memorable events involving my dining room table was upon my husband's and my return from a cruise for our twenty-fifth wedding anniversary. My sisters had come by the house and set up a display on the table that included some beautiful toasting glasses to celebrate, my wedding veil, a wedding picture, and a hat worn by one of my sisters as a bridesmaid. It was a fabulous setup and quite the surprise! —K. Smith

Champagne Punch

2 bottles dry Champagne
2 liters ginger ale
1 (12-ounce) can frozen pink
    lemonade concentrate

1 (14- to 16-ounce) package frozen
    whole strawberries

Combine the Champagne, ginger ale and lemonade concentrate in a large punch bowl and mix well. Add the frozen strawberries just before serving. Ladle into punch cups. Add additional lemonade concentrate for a sweeter flavor. Serves 26 to 28.

For the Love of Oranges

3 or 4 scoops vanilla ice cream
2 cups orange juice

1 cup Champagne

Combine the ice cream, orange juice and Champagne in a blender. Pulse until combined, adding additional ice cream, orange juice and/or Champagne to suit individual tastes. Pour into glasses and serve immediately. Serves 4.

We did not have a dining room table when I was growing up. However, we celebrated all the holidays with my grandparents, aunts, uncles, and cousins at my grandparents' house. As I remember, the dining room table was only used for meals. We gathered for holidays and Sunday dinners. While my children were young, we lived too far away to attend every holiday, but traveled to celebrate Christmas every year for about twenty-five years. Those times together at the dining room table as a family were so special to me that I use my dining table all the time to share everyday moments and special occasions with family and friends. —L. Sewell

Milk Chocolate Chambord Shake

1 cup heavy cream
1 (8-ounce) milk chocolate
    candy bar
3 tablespoons Chambord or other
    raspberry liqueur

1 quart premium vanilla ice cream
1/2 cup milk

Scald the cream in a saucepan. Pour over the chocolate in a heatproof bowl and whisk until combined. Stir in the liqueur. Process the chocolate mixture, ice cream and milk in a blender until smooth. Pour into glasses and serve immediately. Serves 4.

Pomegranate Cocktail

1/2 cup pomegranate juice
2 teaspoons Grand Marnier,
    Cointreau or other
    orange liqueur

1 bottle Prosecco or other dry
    sparking wine, chilled
Pomegranate seeds (optional)

Pour 2 tablespoons of the pomegranate juice and 1/2 teaspoon of the liqueur into each of four Champagne flutes. Fill the flutes with the wine. Garnish with pomegranate seeds. Serves 4.

I dress my dining table and have a centerpiece, candles, etc. I use my dining room and dining room table as a welcome point to the home. We celebrate lots of occasions—birthdays, anniversaries, Christmas, Easter, Thanksgiving, Labor Day, Memorial Day, Fourth of July, Super Bowl, baby showers, and bridal showers. The most memorable are those casual get-togethers where everyone contributes foods and beverages. You get an eclectic array of yummies!
—K. Moore

The Perfect Sangria

1 (750-milliliter) bottle rioja
1/4 cup brandy
1/4 cup sugar
1/4 cup Grand Marnier
2 tablespoons fresh lime juice
2 tablespoons fresh orange juice

1/2 orange, thinly sliced
1/2 lemon, thinly sliced
1/2 lime, thinly sliced
1/2 (375-milliliter) bottle
   sparkling water

Combine all the ingredients except the sparkling water in a large container or pitcher; mix well. Chill, covered, for 2 hours or longer. Add the sparkling water just before serving.

Pomegranate Blueberry Mojito

20 fresh mint leaves
1/2 cup sugar
5 limes
11 ounces pomegranate
   blueberry juice

4 cups fresh limeade
3 cups lemon-lime soda
1/2 to 1 cup white rum
Additional mint leaves (optional)
Blueberries (optional)

This recipe requires 2 hours of refrigeration. Muddle twenty mint leaves with the sugar in a bowl. Extract the juice from the limes using a juicer; discard any pulp. Stir the lime juice into the mint mixture. Chill for 2 hours. Mix the pomegranate blueberry juice, limeade, soda, desired amount of rum and the mint mixture in a large pitcher. Pour over ice in glasses. Garnish with mint leaves and blueberries. Serves 10.

Photograph for this recipe on facing page.

Chocolatier

1/4 cup (2 ounces) chocolate
   ice cream
1 ounce dark Jamaican rum
1/2 ounce crème de cacao

1 1/2 ounces milk
1 tablespoon semisweet
   chocolate shavings

Combine the ice cream, rum, liqueur and milk in a blender. Process at high speed for 10 seconds. Pour over ice in an 8-ounce glass and stir. Sprinkle with the chocolate shavings. Serves 1.

Lake McQueeney Margaritas

12 cups distilled water or
   purified water
4 cups fresh lime juice
   (about 30 large limes)

4 cups premium tequila
2 cups Triple Sec, Grand Marnier
   or Cointreau
2 cups sugar

This recipe requires about 24 hours freezer time. Combine the water, lime juice, tequila, liqueur and sugar in a large round cooler with a spout and mix well. Pour the margarita mixture into large sealable freezer bags and seal tightly. Freeze for about 24 hours for frozen margaritas. Or, serve the margaritas over ice in glasses. Cut the recipe in half, if desired. It keeps well in your freezer and is convenient when friends drop by. The amount of sugar and lime juice may be adjusted according to personal taste. Makes 1 1/2 gallons.

We celebrate traditional holidays and birthdays regularly. Other special occasions are sporadic. The traditional holidays are marked with traditional foods served by both my birth family and my husband's birth family over the years. I have meshed two traditions and menus to create our own traditional dishes. Now our children have these dishes to take with them as they leave home and create their own families. I will be eager to see what foods survive the test of time to the next generation. —L. Martens

Frozen Red Raspberry Margaritas

1 cup water
1 cup sugar
2 cups ice cubes
1 cup red raspberries
1 cup fresh lime juice

1¼ ounces gold tequila
1 ounce Chambord or other
    raspberry liqueur
½ ounce Cointreau or other
    orange liqueur

Bring the water to a boil in a saucepan. Add the sugar and boil until the sugar dissolves. Remove from the heat and let stand until cool.

Combine the sugar syrup, ice cubes, raspberries, lime juice, tequila and liqueurs in a blender. Process until combined, adding additional ice cubes if needed for the desired consistency. Pour into margarita glasses. For sweeter margaritas, increase the Chambord to 1½ ounces. Makes 32 ounces.

Photograph for this recipe on page 90.

Zingy Bloody Mary

16 ounces spicy Bloody Mary mix
    (Zing Zang brand preferred)
3 ounces vodka
½ to ¾ teaspoon horseradish
½ teaspoon Worcestershire sauce
¼ to ½ teaspoon Tabasco sauce

¼ teaspoon celery salt
⅛ teaspoon garlic powder
1 rib celery (optional)
Green olives (optional)
Boiled shrimp (optional)

Combine the Bloody Mary mix, vodka, horseradish, Worcestershire sauce, Tabasco sauce, celery salt and garlic powder in a shaker. Shake and pour over ice in a glass. Garnish with celery, green olives and boiled shrimp. Serves 1.

Vanilla Sugar

It's easy to make vanilla-flavored sugar to top desserts or cocktail glasses. Simply add one vanilla pod to a glass jar or storage container and top with one cup of castor sugar. Let rest for one to two days to allow the flavor to develop into the sugar, shaking occasionally.

Snowflake Martini

3 ounces white cranberry juice
2 ounces blue curaçao
1 ounce vodka
1 piece dry ice

Combine the cranberry juice, liqueur and vodka with ice cubes in a shaker. Shake and pour into one or two martini glasses. Add the dry ice for a smoky effect. Be cautious with the dry ice as it will burn your skin. A small amount will have plenty of effect. Serves 1 or 2.

Photograph for this recipe on facing page.

Pear Martini

6 Bartlett pears
2 tablespoons honey
2 tablespoons fresh lemon juice
1/4 cup water
8 ounces (about) premium vodka
1/2 cup ice cubes
1/4 cup fresh lemon juice
1 teaspoon lemon zest

Peel four of the pears and cut into 1/8-inch slices. Sauté the pear slices in a nonstick skillet for 1 to 2 minutes or just until the slices begin to brown. Remove the pears to a bowl and cool in the refrigerator.

Mix 2 tablespoons honey, 2 tablespoons lemon juice and the water in a bowl. Scoop twelve balls from the remaining two pears using a melon baller and place in the honey mixture, stirring to coat. Marinate for 15 to 30 minutes. Thread three pear balls on each of four skewers.

Combine the sautéed pears, vodka, ice, 1/4 cup lemon juice and the lemon zest in a shaker. Shake vigorously, breaking up the pear slices. Strain into chilled martini glasses, discarding the solids. Garnish each glass with a pear skewer. Serves 4.

Photograph for this recipe on page 230.

Pears

Large, juicy yellow pears are picked in various areas across the state from May until August. Peak production is in June. Consumers will find Texas pears at supermarkets, farmers' markets, roadside stands, and pick-your-own operations.

Underwriters

We wish to graciously thank our generous underwriters for making more room at our table...

Chapter Opener Sponsor

Susan and David Diehl

Community Culinary Contributor

Grape Passion LLC-Fort Worth, Texas, Ivan Thornton, Owner
Vanessa Muse, Prudential Gary Greene Realtors® at www.yourrealtormuse.com

One Thyme Sponsor

Halliburton Giving Choices
Mickey's Travel, Mickey O'Donnell-Owner

Executive Chef

Stacei Bible	Deborah and Jeff Coburn
Ashley Boudreaux	Jodie and Cullen Spitzer
Kathy Nelson Croom	Erin Hanley Bostick
Amy Grace	Jan and Greg Jewell

The 2009–2010 Board
(Bridget Buck, Patty Charles, Carol Durkee, DeAnn Guidry, Jessica Guinn, Missy Herndon,
Carol Lauck, Ali May, Shannon Mills, Jenni Skipper, and Lauren Temple)

Chef de Cuisine

Carol and Todd Durkee
Audra Hoegemeyer

Kathleen Moore
Kristin Lee and Jay Mac Sanders

Sous Chef

Martha Andersen
Lonna and Jon Beamesderfer
Anne Fry
Kallie Gilbreath
Linda Martens

Melissa Mauldin
Jena and Justin McCrann
Shannon and Jason Mills
Amber Oakley
Cheryl Roper Pritzen

Marian Richards
Toni Shepard
Becky Todd
Elaine and Stephen White
Mallory and Matt Yartym

Chef de Partie

Dena and Jerry Beaver
Cheryl and Rick Castagno
Deborah Ann Diehl
Bonnie Jean Diehl
B. Josephine Diehl
Leesa Dodd
Dana Blume DuPlantis
DeAnn Guidry
Rosalyn House
Kathleen and Tom Houser

Yvette Jircik
Janelle Lundy
Rebecca Majewski
Bilinda Matusek
Ali May
Lisa B. McCance
Mary Beth McIver
Laura Minze
Sandra Moon

Vanessa Muse
Natalie Keller Nance
Denise Schiel
Kelly Shearer
Luann W. Tietze
Cindy Tilley
Theresa Wagaman
Kacy Yarbro
Bren Yeager
2008–2009 Provisional Class

Acknowledgments

For every place setting you designed to make our table inviting...

Photography

Terry Vine Photography
For your incredible eye and vision to help bring this project to life.

Food Stylist

Julie Hettiger
For creating delectable food styling, creative direction, and endless commitment.

Junior League Liaison and Prop Stylists

Laura Baxter Cannetti
Alison Peters Henderson
Melanie King Interior Designs
For artistic creativity and cohesive design for every photograph in this collection.

Props

Retailers

abellaboutique.com
Eklektic Interiors
House Sweet It Is
Kuhl-Linscomb
Potter's Wheel Gallery and Gifts
Tristiani

From their homes to our table

Lonna Beamesderfer	Susan T. Diehl	Whitney McCoy
Ashley Boudreaux	Carol Durkee	Jena McCrann
Kim Bradley	Alison Peters Henderson	Shannon Mills
Laura Baxter Cannetti	Jan Jewell	Carmina Robuck
Kathy Nelson Croom	Melanie King	Kristin Lee Sanders
Julie Crum		

For the unconditional use of all of your beautiful and unique pieces that adds the extra touch in making the food shine.

Florals

The Blooming Idea, The Woodlands, Texas
HEB
For elegant florals that added the finishing touch to our tables

Photography Locations

Carol and Calvin Cobb
Carol and Russell Fryman
Becky and Mark Lanier
Coco and Kelly Mahoney
Marian and Dan Spence
Honey and Rex Tucker
Thank you to each homeowner for allowing us to photograph in your beautiful homes

Special Thanks

Lonna Beamesderfer
Cara Canovas
Karen Carroll
Chick-Fil-A, The Woodlands/Magnolia
JL Communications Team—Missy Herndon, Yvette Brum Williams, and Prisilla Vinson
Creative Concepts Printing, Graphics, and Design
Carol Durkee
Shannon Mills
Jamie Hartwell Zigrang
woodlandsonline.com
For all that you did behind the scenes

For sustaining the team on location

Elva Akin	Susan T. Diehl	Jan Jewell
Sallie Ben Barlow	Libby George	Ali May
Bridget Buck	DeAnn Guidry	Carol McHorse
Presha Carr	Missy Herndon	Jenni Skipper
Kris Conner	Audra Hoegemeyer	Sandy Smith

We would like to especially thank the families of the wives and mothers
who spent countless hours on the phone, in the kitchen, at the market, and at meetings
to develop this gift for all of our supporters.

Development Committee

Cookbook Committee Chair
Susan Tegethoff Diehl

Sustaining Advisor
Jan Jewell

Assistant Chair
Laura Miller

Administrative Assistant
DeAnn Guidry

Recipe Co-Chairs
Ashley Boudreaux   Kathy Nelson Croom

Recipe Coordinators
Melissa Mauldin   Elaine Pereira White
Jena Ryder McCrann   Mallory Yartym

Art, Design, and Editorial Co-Chairs
Amy Grace   Kristin Lee Sanders

Marketing Co-Chairs
Kathleen Moore   Toni Shepard

Underwriting Co-Chairs
Erin Hanley-Bostick   Kathleen Houser

Cookbook Sales
Tamara Leigh   Pilar Middleton   Penny Sampler

Presidents

Julie Gilbert	Audra Hoegemeyer	Shannon Mills
2007–2008	2008–2009	2009–2010

Mission Statement

The Junior League of North Harris and South Montgomery Counties, Inc., is an organization of women committed to promoting voluntarism, developing the potential of women, and improving communities through the effective action and leadership of trained volunteers. Its purpose is exclusively educational and charitable.

Recipe Contributors and Testers

Elva Akin
Holly Anderson
Martha Andersen
Nicole Peterek Anderson
Ruth Anderson
Tiffany Hjornevik Baker
Charla Weeks Balette
Erika Sudderth Barker
Sallie Ben Barlow
Darcy Bass
Lonna Beamesderfer
Dena Fraini Beaver
Sharon Bell
Inger Berger
Sally Bierman
Allison Wallace Blake
Erin Blank
Pam Boren
Erin Hanley Bostick
Allyson Boudousquie
Ashley Boudreaux
Regina Bowen
John Brazie
Allison Brighten
Kandy Brun
Cheryl Bryan
Kay Buccautimi
Bridget Buck
Lindsey Buerger
Jennifer Bulovas
Lisa Burlas
Brooke Keitz Burns
Holly Byrd
Susan Cain
Laura Baxter Cannetti

Cara Canovas
Barbara Calhoun Cargill
Presha Carr
Karen Carroll
Cheryl Castagno
Patty Charles
Katie Clymer
Carol Cobb
Deborah Cornwall Coburn
Jessica Cofas
Caroline Crawford
Casie Crawford
Lisa Edris Crichton
Kathy Nelson Croom
Julie Crum
Liz Curtin
Karen Deilke
Michele De La Garza
Julia Dell
Jacqueline Mortiz Dewese
Susan Tegethoff Diehl
Deneé Dimiceli
Wendy Greer DiPasquale
Kim Dodson
Tracy Downham
Vicki Downing
Melissa Doyle
Kathryn Driskill
Estella D'Souza
Carol Durkee
Kathy Durnil
Bethany Johnson Dylewski
Dawn Emmons-Hynes
Leigh Ann Engibous
Margaret Falkenhagen

Karen Falterman
Beverly Fincher
Tonya Fletcher
Cindy Siokos Foley
Barbara Foxhall
Linda Froelich
Carol Fryman
Russ Fryman
James Garon
Dana Gary
Shelly Gault
Kallie Shivers Gilbreath
Michelle Kaye Gilmore
Debbie Godbold
Ami Goedke
Emily Gogineni
Jo Ann Goldman
Alexis Goodson
Sasicha Goodwin
Amy Grace
Sharon Gressett
Jeanette Grau
Jennifer Grigsby
DeAnn Guidry
Candi Thibodeaux Guilbeau
Bianca Hadjioannou
Meghan Hadjioannou
Dina Hafley
Jennifer Hammonds
Kathie Heath
Cindy Heiser
Alison Peters Henderson
Cara Henderson
Jeanette Henry
Brandi Williams Herman

recipe contributors and testers continued

Missy Herndon
Tracy Hird
Audra Wells Hoegemeyer
Rachael Leah Holland
Anna Hollier
Cindy Holmes
Rachel Honeyman
Jan Hopkins
Sue Hubbard
Colbie Hubenak
Jennie Hughes
Lauretta Hynes
Kathy Igercich
Heather Jackson
Stacey Cheshire Jeter
Jan Foster Jewell
Deanne Johnson
Rebecca Johnson
Kristin Jones
Sheila Jortner
Alison Judge
Leigh Kamasz
Nikki Keith
Lisa Krenek Kelley
Nicole Kenisky
Tia Kennedy
Michelle Keyes
Amy S. Killingsworth
Diana Kilponen
Melanie King
Kasie Kline
Lacey Knoll
Michele Weaver Kooken
Rhonda Kovich
Wendy Kovich
Tritia Land

Kellie Lange
Sue Lassinger
Heather LeBlanc
Amy LeCrone
Tamara Leigh
Leesa Lemon
Natalie Leslie
Julie Lewandowski
Denise Lipar
Stephanie Locklear
Gail Lockwood
Melissa Londa
Mary Lostak
Aida Lotts
Linda Martens
Karen Martin
Liz Martin
Amanda Mason
Melissa Mauldin
Ali and Randy May
Nancy McConnell
Whitney McCoy
Jena Ryder McCrann
Carol Augustine McHorse
Pippa McLennan
Trisha McLeod
Laetatia McMullin
Mary Ellen Schellang Michel
Harriet Mikkelson
Ann Miller
Christy Miller
Laura Miller
Meredith Miller
Tara Miller
Robbin Mills
Shannon Mills

Tava Miya
Ann Mohr
Deborah Mohr
Kathleen Moore
Sherry Moore
Samy Morcos
Stacey Morcos
Diana Morrow
Nicole Murphy
Vanessa Sudderth Muse
Coleman Mobley Nalley
Caryl Ann Nelson
Jauveda Acuff Netherton
Paula Newton
Debra Norman
Vicki Norrell
Amber Oakley
Cara O'Leary
Tracey O'Neal
Janice Owens
Laura Lea Palmer
Michelle Peacock
Dave Pennington
Elizabeth Pereira
Chrissy Pickett
Karen Pickett
Lori Cunningham Pinto
Clancy Plaisance
Susan Planting
Lisa Podraza
Janie Price
Cheryl R. Pritzen
Julie Pruski
Kristen Rabel
Kirsten Graham Randolph
Kelly Reed-Hirsch

Joyce Reynolds
Jennifer Richard
Nettie LeBlanc Richardson
Jamie Riley
Andrea Rucker
Sondra Rekuc Ruhman
Denise Russo
Penny Warren Sampler
Jerrie Ann Sanders
Kristin Lee Sanders
Julie Sansbury
Tracy Santoro
Trista M. Baumboree Savoy
Denise Schiel
Louise Schulter
Bill Sealy
Jacqueline Sealy
Betsy Sebastian
Lisa Segelquist
Lee Ann Sewell
Wilma Sewell
Kelly Shearer
Jennifer Sheehan
Toni Shepard
Faith Shipp
Melba Shipp
Jennie Shirley
Debbie Silver
Gay Michel Simmons
Terri Simmons
Jenni Skipper
Molly Slagle
Craig Smith
Louise Smith
Sandy Smith
Casey Snyder

Adria Stacha
Tava Stanford
Melissa Stanosheck
Trigg Stock
Judith Magnell Stone
Melissa Strathman
Susan Sweeten Strobl
Pam Sullivan
Erika Olivares Sumner
Lauren Temple
Amy Thedinger
Margaret Thornton
Cindy Tilley
Jane Tinsley
Suzanne Todd
Gaye Cline Tonroy
Christine Touchstone
Paula Trahan
Marybeth Twellman
Misty Twellman
Samantha Urbanek
Amy Vandervoot
Michelle Vando
Priscilla Butler Vinson
Theresa Wagaman
Martha Walker
Becky Wall
Ashley Wallace
Angela Waters
Kathy Watkins
Sarah Watson
Jeanne Trapani Watts
Meredith Patton Watts
Patricia Wells
Christi Wetzel
Elaine Pereira White

John Lindsay White
Linda White
Pam White
Stephen Robert White
Hannah Whitlock
Norris Whitlock
Sandy Whitlock
Abby Whitmire
Dianne White Wilcox
Yvette Brun Williams
Brandi Williamson
Kimberly Willing
Coosh Willis
Eva Wolf
Kelley Wolf
Donna Wright
Mallory Yartym
Betty Young
Bonnie Young
Evelyn Young
Kathleen Young
Marnie Young
Marsha L. Muecke Young

Index

Texas Tables

Texas Tables